Ten Boxes

A STORY OF STUFF

by
Susan Fekete

Susan Fekete

Santa Rosa, California

Published by
Susan Fekete
PO Box 14122
Santa Rosa, CA 95402
www.susanfekete.com
www.ten-boxes.com

Acknowledgement is made to the following:

© Longreads (2018) Susan Fekete
Portions of this work first published in Longreads.

ISBN 978-0-692-08651-3 (hardcover)
ISBN 978-0-692-08601-8 (paperback)
ISBN 978-0-692-08602-5 (eBook)

Edited by Gail Westerfield
Collage art by Riikka Fransila
Cover design by Kat Mellon

Ten Boxes

A STORY OF STUFF

CHAPTER 1

Things

B y the time I was six years old, I knew what a tobacco barn was. And a hornet's nest. And the difference between hyacinth and hydrangea. I knew that a duck wasn't a duck, but a mallard, a wood duck, a merganser. I also had already learned that ducks can, and will, bite. By the age of eight, I knew the difference between grosgrain and satin, denim and chambray. By ten, I'd been taught the difference between pickling and canning, and what a harvest moon was, and why it wasn't the same as a full moon. By fourteen, I'd learned what clear definitions of "consciousness," "responsibility," "choice," and "accountability" were.

All my life, my mother taught me to use language, to learn names, to describe life as it is, honestly and without hesitation. She gave me words and the power to discern, define, detail, delineate.

Driving south on US 27: "That's grapefruit, probably white."

Two miles later. "Tangerines."

"How can you tell?"

"They look different."

"Duh. Yeah. One's yellow, one's orange."

"Smarty pants."

She eased the car to the shoulder. I sighed.

This, you see, was the point in any of my "education" sessions when always, if I knew best, I should sigh and resign myself that just about anything was about to happen – and the only guaranteed factor in the equation was that it was going to somehow involve me. And her. Five minutes later, we might be chatting with a citrus farmer or traipsing willy-nilly through the groves in search of other species. Or sketching a picture of a tree on a fast food napkin retrieved from the glove compartment. There was no telling. It was to be an adventure.

An adventure! I also learned early in life that many words held multiple meanings, depending on your perspective on the word. "Adventure" could be a quick stop-off at the one and only Dairy Inn within a 30-mile radius of Frostproof, Florida, in order to experience the true glory of a properly executed peanut butter milkshake. However, let's be clear: Odds were 50/50, so it was just as likely that the adventure might be following a dirt road – in a car with no spare tire and very little gasoline –

to some arts festival that she was sure she had heard about, which was, she was sure, this weekend.

Need I go on? Peanut butter shake: delicious. Out of gas in the middle of fucking nowhere in Florida during a raging thunderstorm: not so delicious.

All I'm saying here is that it was, to be sure, always a gamble. And always an adventure – just sometimes a better, easier adventure than others. I'm really pretty sure that it was in the grand design of things that my mom lived the vast majority of her years in a time before everyone had cell phones with cameras and YouTube and Twitter. Eccentrics make excellent fodder for viral videos and my mom was plexiglass: tough, resilient, transparent – and the wrong blow could run a crack through her that would never disappear.

"Seriously," I said, staring at the grove. "How can you tell? There's no fruit on the trees."

"They look different."

"Citrus trees." I feigned disinterest. (I was always interested in what she had to say.)

"They look different. Look at them. Look."

"I'm looking."

"Look at the size of the tree. The color of the leaves. The shape of the branches. You've got to take time to get to know the world you live in. Little things can matter a lot. Look at these trees."

I did, and she went down the road a piece, and I looked at some more trees. And further – more trees. And I learned. I learned to call them by name, to be precise, why each was special, and why each was different. I learned why names mattered. And though she wasn't always good at it, sometimes she could even pull up from memory some thin bit of Latin that might just be the root word that something or other about the tree or plant or fruit or soil came from.

I learned what a hard freeze would do. How farmers could cross-breed trees. (The real way, the old way – not some laboratory GMO Frankenplant that we really didn't even know about yet.) And on and on. One day. One trip. A two-hour drive to my grandmother's house that ended up taking three-and-a-half. Only a tiny, tiny part of why my mom was always late.

I could tell the difference between a strawberry crop, a tomato crop, a cucumber crop, a soybean crop, or a snap pea crop from about as far away as any farmer. My mother taught me to look, to care. She taught me to somehow give a nod of respect to the thing itself by having a word for it, knowing how to call it, to recall it, to share it.

"What a beautiful patch of pansies and petunias," she'd say. "What a royal amethyst color," instead of a simple, "What pretty purple flowers." Everything was shared. Everything a lesson.

No wonder she kept things.

I mean she kept things. Stuff. Items. Mountains of them.

So there's a small difficulty, I've found, in telling her story – or stories about her. It's called "reality television." Anyone who abhors most of it in the way that I do will understand . . . well, you already do. For the rest of you, those who actually tune in regularly to view with detachment the grim sadness of others' televised lives, I may need to explain:

Reality television is not real. And please don't nod your head and ignore this paragraph as something you already know, as dismissive as a young girl of an orange tree. Think about how un-real it all is. When you watch an episode – or, God forbid, every episode – of "Storage Wars" or "Gold Rush" or "Real Housewives," you need to step way, way, way, way back. Don't look into the lights. Don't be dazzled by the fierce mundanity of it all. Step back and realize how little you care about anything that is going on. It will not affect the way you sleep tonight or rise tomorrow. It will not affect your checkbook, your presence at the next homeowners' association meeting, your children's acceptance into college, your hair color, the length of your hem (unless you're watching "Project Runway"), or anything else about the very real people and places that are a part of your very real life. Reality. Your reality. Not TV's.

(I'd also like to offer a sidebar here: I'd love to discuss whether I misspoke in the paragraph above with anyone who has the data. I'm afraid it may, in fact, be true that there is a direct correlation between your children's acceptance into the college of their choice and whether you watched "Jersey Shore." Just maybe.)

I'm saying that unless you are the parent, spouse, or child of a hoarder, stop here for a moment. Take a breath and forget everything television ever told you about "hoarding." It's this decade's popular mental illness, which will be replaced next decade by another. You might think you know something about it from television. Or an article in a doctor's office magazine. Maybe even a documentary, if you're the bleeding-heart, Netflix late-at-night-alone type (like I am, sometimes). Still, I beg you. For the sake of my mom's memory – forget what you think you know.

My mom kept things.

CHAPTER 2

Buttons

I'm a few years older than I was the last time I thought much about my mom's stuff. I think about it a little every time I move. I think about it when I break something that I regard as valuable. I spent a great deal of time, years ago, thinking about when it all began and why I didn't notice. But it wasn't until just recently – days ago, really – that I began to remember her piles of stuff from my childhood. I had somehow pushed out of my head, perhaps by willpower alone, the place where her stuff was.

The stuff in the garage.

The garage was a place I didn't go much when I was a child. No one did. I remember playing in the garage, just a little, maybe on a few rainy days when I was very, very young. By the time I was eight, I'm not even sure if a person could have gotten into the garage. T.C.'s stuff was in there. T.C.'s stuff was now my mom's. Imagine.

Thomas Celestine – T.C. for short – was my maternal grandfather: from what I've heard tell, my abusive, alcoholic, manic-depressive (we didn't call it "bipolar disorder" then) grandfather. T.C. had been an auto mechanic, ran a shop of his own, for pretty much as long as my mom could remember. T.C. used to sit, sometimes for days or weeks on end, in the dark. Or lie down. He'd disappear into his bedroom one afternoon or evening and not reappear until the murky, undeniable fog of gloom had lifted again from his heart. I'm not sure what they called depression in the early 1940s, if they called it anything at all. My mom and her siblings knew not to trifle with him. It was best to leave him alone, unless he called for them – for a glass of water or another bottle of bourbon. He didn't eat. He slept. And sat. And stared. Until he would, one day, for no known reason, rise from his bed, shower and shave, and greet the world anew.

I imagine no one considered it "bipolar," either, when he burst into the children's rooms at night, long after bedtime, throwing on the overhead lights and bellowing for them to "Get up!" They were going to take a ride. Or go on a trip. Or clean the house. Apparently, his exuberance was as random as his sobriety, and as unpredictable as his recovery from gloom. His behavior certainly showed in my mom, or, perhaps I should say, in her habits. For example, she hated overhead lights all my life. She'd fill a room with floor lamps and table lamps, but she would not turn on an overhead light unless something great was at stake.

My grandmother had taken her five children and left T.C. when my mom was only seven. Grandmother headed south out of the Indiana farms and the coal mines of Kentucky for the golden promise of Florida's sun, where she waitressed in a diner on the beach and raised her kids as well as she could, alone. T.C. followed her some time later, all the way to Florida, and, several boyfriends later, Grandmother married him again, had more kids. Then divorced him again. And then she died. And then he died . . . leaving behind all of his stuff.

My mom was the obvious one – perhaps the only one – to bear the burden of her father's stuff. By the time T.C died, the living children in the family numbered seven. (There had been others. Miscarriages – at least two. There was another child, stillborn, nameless in our recorded history. There was also a girl who mom always referred to as "Baby Margaret," who died very, very young. I think she was born with a hole in her heart. At least, that's what I remember being told. Years later, though, I found old journals written by my mom. There was one page that talked about T.C. and the "drunken beatings" my grandmother endured from his hands. That same entry referred to "the bloody death of baby Margaret" and I have since always wondered what she meant. I never asked.)

When T.C. died, Mom's two older brothers – Marvin and Bo – were many miles away, both with families and concerns of their own. Mom was still in St. Pete, married, and she was already keeping a roof over the heads of the younger four children.

My mom and dad, following the death of my grandmother, took in as "wards" her two brothers – Jerry and Charlie – and one sister, Becky, who were not old enough to fend for themselves. Another sister, Linda, old enough but perhaps not ready yet to take on the world alone, came along for the wild ride. It's a damned good thing she did. She, and later my aunt Becky, were the desperately needed second pair of hands that life gave to my mom for many years. Not only were they hands, they were level heads in a sea of tumult. If you're from a family full of addicts and eccentrics, you know how essential just one tiny island of anything that feels like "normal" can be.

My parents' young lives transformed, almost overnight. By the time they'd been married just two years, they had a newborn baby of their own, plus an insta-family of four other young souls to care for, educate, feed, and bathe. Then T.C. died, and they got his stuff. Bonus.

When he died, I was really young. Four, I think. I don't remember him at all. I once thought that I remembered him: I had an image in my head from an old photo of a man in a chair. I thought it was T.C. until I was a teenager and discovered it was actually another relative entirely. Then, a few weeks ago, I came across a photo of a man I didn't recognize. He wore glasses, had a sharp nose and an all-business, straightforward gaze that gave nothing away. On the back, in my mom's handwriting: "T.C., about 18." During my life, she never called him "Dad," or "Father." No "Papa," no term of endearment. He was T.C., always T.C. and only T.C., which spoke volumes.

So I really don't remember him at all. But I remember his stuff. I remember his shop. Spark plug signs and the smell of axle grease. Racks and racks of parts I didn't understand. Little pieces in little drawers, big hoses on the wall. Stacks upon stacks of air filters in dusty boxes. My mom taught me "fan belt" and "radiator," "nut" and "bolt," but that was about as far as she could go.

Mom knew nothing about cars. In fact, by the way she treated most of her vehicles in life, I believe she may have secretly hated cars. Maybe that's how she kept her karma even with T.C. – by truly fucking up all the cars she ever owned. Royally. Ignoring them, cracking blocks, seizing brakes. Not attending to their most basic needs – like water, gas, and oil – or to the lights that come on when you don't attend to them. She barely even took the time to look at her gas gauge, as evidenced by the memories – more than I can count – of walking, gas can in hand, to the nearest gas station from wherever we'd had to abandon our vehicle. Maybe it was all a great big unconscious payback for life giving her a shitty dad. Anyway, I think that the only parts she could name were the ones that had already gone wrong, that had blown up in, or fallen off of, a car she'd owned at one point or other.

So there's my mom, and there's all this stuff. My parents were raising, by the time T.C. died, seven children. And there's a garage full of stuff that's got to have some value to it. Right? Auto parts are expensive. We should be able to sell them somehow. The road to my mother's own private hoarding hell was, indeed, paved with good intentions, the very best.

So my mom kept T.C.'s stuff. It went straight out of T.C.'s garage and into ours. And it stayed there.

My mom was frugal. Born in 1939, she'd been taught to be. Her grandmother saved aluminum foil. She told my mom that children couldn't drink (then-rationed) coffee because it would turn them black (something that you didn't much want to be in Kentucky, or anywhere else, during the early 1940s). Things had value and needed to be saved, reused, repurposed, repaired. Things could be sold. One didn't just throw away a thing if it had value. It had a name.

We moved out of that house when I was ten years old. By then, there was more stuff.

There seemed to be some correlation between how much empty space my mom had in any home, how many people occupied said home, and how much stuff she could shove into the home without appearing to the outside world to be mad as a hatter. Her children were growing: Her firstborn was off to the Air Force, and her youngest had long since vacated the nursery. Even Linda had moved on, all the way across the country to California. (Talk about needing some space!) What better place for a new sewing room than an old nursery?

Now, did she use the sewing room? Sure she did! I was one of the best-dressed little girls in the parish on the last Friday of each month, when we got to leave our plaid jumpers and white blouses with Peter Pan collars at home and have "Dress Up Day" at St. Paul's Catholic School. I had a new outfit every month. Gingham, seersucker, paisley. Gored skirts, A-line, prairie style. Granted, the outfit would have been finished that very same morning, as I wolfed down my breakfast, and then was hemmed while being worn, in the car on the way to school.

"Arvin, slow down a little."

Dad didn't usually drive us to school. For a lot of my early life, I think he was already at work by the time I was headed out the door in the morning. First a baggage handler, then a salesman, and later a ticket agent, for Greyhound Bus Lines, back when taking the bus was still both a viable and desirable mode of transportation, Dad often was at work in the early morning hours. Later, driving a taxi, he was often just getting into bed as I was getting up. Or that's how I remember it. Sounds pretty nose-to-the-grindstone, hard-workin', all-American. That wasn't exactly how some would describe my dad, so

I'm sure there's much more to it all than I remember.

"I'm only doing the speed limit."

"I know. But slow down a little. I'm not quite done."

I heaved a heavy sigh. We were only four blocks from my school, and Mom had broken her thread and was now trying to re-thread a needle as Dad navigated down the bumpy red brick road.

"Maybe you should pull over," she said.

"I'm gonna be late *again*!" I whined.

"I know. I'll write you a note."

"I don't want another note. I'm *always* late!"

Dad intervened. "Hold on, Suzie. Just a few minutes, and your mom will be done with your *pretty new dress*."

That was his reminder. Not only was I about to speak out of turn to one of my parents, which wasn't tolerated well in our home, but I was also about to behave like an ingrate by not considering the several hours of sleep that my mom had lost the night before as she constructed said garment, *and* a matching one for my favorite teddy bear, Andrusa. My dad didn't always have a lot to say, but he sure as hell meant what he did say. Usually. Unless he was lying. But that's another story.

The clock never ticked faster as minutes raced by. I fidgeted inside. I kept my mouth shut. I thought about the long, long aisle between desks, counting the pairs of eyes watching me. (*That Susan*

– *she's* always *late!*) But they would still give me valentines. They would still play four-square with me. I would go to their birthday parties, and they to mine, but they still watched when I came in late, and I was dead sure that they all knew what a disaster – train wreck, tornado, act of God – my mother was, that I really didn't *want* to be late but was a slave to her creativity. A peacock impatiently waiting for its perfectly painted, luminescent feathers to grow. Tick-tick-tick-tick . . . tock.

She finished.

I was late.

And my dress was PERFECT.

It was pretty. So pretty. Everything she ever made for me was pretty. And special. She would spend hours going through buttons until she found just the right ones: little golden bears for one dress, white plastic bunnies for another, and mother-of-pearl scallops for the jumper with seashells on it. She'd spend an extra hour once everything looked finished just to hand-sew three rows of bric-a-brac around the sleeves. She'd take twice as long cutting out a pattern because she had to use four different fabrics to colorblock something the way she wanted. (Yes, my mom was colorblocking before fashion knew what that meant!) When it was finally finished, it would be stunning. The question was always and only *when* it would be finished.

Mom didn't do many things in advance. Or on time, really. Ever. But she did them. The sewing room was used – and filled with good intentions, one bolt of fabric at a time. There were the countless yards for new drapes she planned to sew, but those were forgotten when a few yards for school Christmas pageant angel costumes were thrown on top of them. There were boxes and boxes and baby food jars full of buttons: mother of pearl buttons by the pint, coconut shell buttons for a whole Polynesian island, plastic buttons and Bakelite buttons, rhinestone buttons, glass buttons, and wooden buttons in every shape and color a child's mind could imagine. There were countless spools of thread – some cotton, some polyester, and "every child should be taught the difference."

The sewing room was useful, productive, and full of promise, full of projects, full of hope. Then it became just full. The bolts of fabric – satin, cotton, double-knit – atop one another began to form barricades and landslides. The heaps of patterns became dry mounds of fire hazard. All the promise of projects to be realized was buried under more hope, more anticipation, more desire . . . more stuff. By the time we left that house, the sewing room could not be negotiated without climbing up a couple of feet and belly-crawling across the mound. Actually *moving* the mound was a feat of Olympic proportion, and a scene that neighbors turned out of their homes and stood on their lawns to watch. Not to help: to watch.

Our home, you see, was a big two-story with a walk-in attic. Five bedrooms – six, if you counted the attic, seven, if you counted the extra room off our dining room. Not fancy. Just big. Full of people and full of stuff. I think that both Aunt Becky and my brothers were fairly clear that Mom had reached some sort of breaking point, perhaps a point of no return, during this move.

Years later, Mom would tell me that my father never lifted a finger during that move. I don't know if that was entirely true, but it certainly could have been.

My father's story is a different book. He came fresh out of the Florida orange groves in a handsome package, as full of trouble as a Minneola is full of juice. The burden of his troubles wasn't stuff – or, it *was*, but his stuff came in the form of tiny, identically shaped tablets. Capsules. Pills. Prescriptions. They could be carried in his pocket, briefcase, glove compartment. He, much like my grandfather, had a tendency to disappear into a cool, dark, closed room when things got strange. Or another woman's bed. Or just somewhere that was not-at-home.

As I said, his is another story. And don't you dare reduce him to some asshole on an episode of "Cheaters." He was much more complex than that.

They were.

It all is.

Reality? Check. This was my reality.

The 26-foot moving truck had been filled and emptied twice, and the belongings continued to pour out of the house. Finally, in a fit of frustration and anger, Mom threw open the windows of the second-floor sewing room and opened bed sheets onto the sloped roof. Before any of us knew what was really happening, boxes of books and garbage bags full of fabric began sliding down the roof and falling with a thud into our front yard. The boxes of books split open on occasion, their syllables cascading across our lawn: Edgar Cayce, Carlos Castaneda, Merriam-Webster, and the "Illustrated Medical Dictionary." Muslin and corduroy burst bags at the seams, and tiny jars of pea-sized buttons went spilling across the not-grass.

It frightened me.

Even at that age, I could predict that a huge box full of heavy books dropping from a second-story ledge would likely burst open when it hit the ground 12 or so feet below. Why could my mother not? THAT scared me.

I'd later come to understand that I was still connected to my mother's heartbeat, still very in tune with the ebb and flow of her body's circadian rhythms. What scared me wasn't boxes or books. What scared me was her fury, her upset, her confusion, her suffocation. What scared me was watching her flounder. What scared me was where *she* went when everything else – the madness – took over. It is, I believe, perhaps only by the grace of God that I did not see my mom's madness clearly then, nor for many years to come.

I'd like to take a moment here to talk about the words I choose to use. I'm entirely aware that "madness" is not a politically correct term for mental illness. Neither are "crazy" or "nuts," and "berserk" generally doesn't go over well either. I acknowledge and respect anyone coping with mental illness, in their own lives or the lives of those they love. My mom *was*, around what we all hope will be our midlife, diagnosed as having bipolar disorder. It likely plagued her for years, even decades, before diagnosis. But I am not writing only about my mom's mental illness; I am writing about my mom, the whole of her: the good choices and the absolutely terrible choices. The insights as well as the complete self-deceit and blindness. The depth of her honesty as well as the vastness of her lies. So when I refer to her madness, her craziness, her eccentricities, I am not referring to her mental health alone. I am referring to the whole, the humanness of her exceedingly *human* condition.

Not everything that spun out of control was because she was bipolar. Executing the demands of one's madness is sometimes a choice, and my mother was not one to play the victim. She was a very beautiful, creative, intelligent being with a biochemical disorder, and she was also sometimes mad as a hatter. So, please, don't hunt me down and tell me that I should be more politically correct.

These are *my* goddamned shoes. I have worn them for miles and miles, across the country and around the globe. I will tell you whether they fit.

CHAPTER 3

Irked

For a long time, I sort of forgot what happened to the stuff. I remembered moving a *lot* of stuff out of our house, but I couldn't remember moving it *to* anywhere. I think I'd imagined (read: hoped) it was donated to some worthy cause, or maybe just thrown away.

The house we moved to when I was ten years old was tiny by comparison to the home I'd known until then. The attic was a tiny space above our ceiling with a square hole that you had to access by dragging a ladder into the house and climbing up. It had barely enough space for luggage, let alone much stuff. Nothing like the long, creaking wooden stairway that led up to the finished attic in our old house, where more than one of us longed to stake our claim and say, "This is my room." That attic room had been my uncle Jerry's, mostly, in the end. It was cool, weird, fun, and just a little creepy. It smelled like old, unpolished wood and generally only gave me goosebumps if I was alone there at night. Family cats escaped to the quiet there to bear litters inside of abandoned suitcases. It was the first place I experienced "sacred" and "spooky" simultaneously. That may not seem so odd, but remember: I was Catholic.

Our new house had only three bedrooms. It had no garage in which to store T.C.'s stuff, just a carport and a shed. That was it. Still, it's amazing how much stuff can be piled into a carport.

When we left the big house, only Mom's car – a Ford Pinto – went into the carport at the new house. Dad's giant pastel yellow Lincoln Continental filled the driveway until he moved out. It seemed, with the exception of a small pile in the corner of my parents' room, that the stuff was gone. I remember being sad, a little, but feeling so free. I was so happy that nothing we owned smelled of axle grease.

I, like my mom, hated the terrazzo floors in our new house and wanted our old screened porch back, but I didn't miss the stuff. I wished we still lived in a quiet neighborhood instead of having our front door face 16th Street, a four-lane thoroughfare, but I didn't consciously miss the rooms that could not be entered because they were filled with stuff.

It wasn't until several months later that I learned where all of it had gone.

We were out on a Saturday adventure, my mom and I. This particular day's big plans entailed picking up her paycheck and going to the bank to cash it, stopping at a few yard sales, going to the "scratch and dent" grocery to see what deals we would find there, and going by a local lake with some two-day-old bread (from the scratch and dent store) to feed the ducks (mallards, mergansers.) On the way home, as I busily stuffed one empty bread bag inside of another in the passenger seat, she announced, "I have to make a quick stop."

I was only ten years old, but the words "quick stop" were already as meaningful to me as the low rumble of thunder across Tampa Bay when a lightning storm was moving in.

A quick stop meant "Be prepared to sit in the car."

A quick stop meant that a great deal of business was to be transacted, or a great number of words were to be shared, all of which was thought to be far too "adult" to concern me.

A quick stop meant I'd soon be singing to myself, tying and retying my shoelaces, or buckling and unbuckling my sandals to pass the time, drawing pictures in the nearby sand or dirt or anthill with a stick. And sweating. Stopping to do anything in Florida usually meant sweating. Making a quick stop to do anything during the daytime in the summer on the vinyl seats of a Ford Pinto definitely meant sweating. I have always sweated a great deal, much more than is becoming to a young lady, but I've never been very good at it. I don't tolerate it well. I get grumpy. Miserable. I don't look good sweaty, regardless of what one all-too-horny boyfriend would have had me believe. I don't get a natural/healthy/just-exercised glow. I sweat *profusely*, my face gets red, my clothes stick to every surface on my body, and my hair flattens and drags, stick-straight. I don't love it; I don't want to make it happen, hence my unhealthy aversion to exercise for much of my life.

So, a heretofore unannounced "quick stop" was never a welcome sidetrack. On this occasion, the quick stop would further educate me in the ways of stuff. And storage.

The place we pulled up to was in an alley – the back of a house somewhere in the northeast section of town. The garage was funny to me; it wasn't like ours had been. It ran the entire length of the property line and had tall doors that looked like they belonged on a barn. It looked like the garage was two stories high, because there was an apartment above it, but from the alley you couldn't tell, so it looked like the tallest garage I'd ever seen.

I don't remember whether my mom went to the door, but I do remember that she and the old red-headed lady talked for a very long time. The lady came out into the alley in her muumuu, and I remember thinking that my mom must've awakened her because her hair looked like a briar patch, tumbleweed, bird's nest. (I spent a few minutes turning my shoelaces into birds' nests before listening to Mom and the lady talking.)

I knew that the red-headed lady was angry. She wasn't yelling or causing a scene, but her too-slow and far-too-controlled speech was familiar. She was lecturing, even if I couldn't hear what she was lecturing about. I felt awkward, like I didn't want to be there. I wasn't yet accustomed to the idea that my parents weren't the be-all-end-all authority on all things. To hear my own mother being chastised, admonished, given what-for was incongruous with nearly everything I understood about power structure. Worse was stopping to wonder what she'd done.

I'm sure at some point I had to pee and made it known, and was told "just a few more minutes" more than once. Maybe I only remember it because it was as memorable as finding a treasure chest full of dung, but I remember that this particular quick stop took FOR . . . E . . . VER.

The lady at some point opened one of the big barn doors. I couldn't figure out what was going on until I started to recognize the things inside . . . the stuff. It was our stuff. T.C.'s stuff. Mom's stuff. Dozens upon dozens of boxes of books. Fabric. Car parts. Furniture. Flowerpots. Stuff.

This is where it went.

Suddenly everything fell – dominoes – into place as I looked at the stuff, the lady, my mom. Turned out, the several carloads full that had magically disappeared in our move to the busy-street, terrazzo-floored house had suddenly reappeared before me, in the barn door garage of an angry tumbleweed head. Turned out, several months before, my mom had made an agreement to pay the woman a monthly amount to safekeep our stuff. Mom filled up the space, and then simply disappeared and quit returning phone calls. The lady was kind enough not to simply throw it all away, but still expected some cash for all those months of storage. Now, this may not have been the first, but it was certainly one of the most glaring demonstrations of my mom's enormous capacity to break promises with all the best intentions.

I still am not entirely certain whether that particular lot of stuff was recovered from the lady. I don't know if those very bits of our past were the selfsame bits I'd trip across again and again in the future. It could be that the books in that garage were the same ones piled in her living room the last time I dug her out of it.

Before we drove away that day, I remember the tumbleweed saying to Mom, "Jonelle, you have irked me. Irked me to the core."

I've never forgotten that sentence. I don't know who I told, or maybe one of my brothers was sitting in the car with me that day as my mother was regressed to childhood and chastised for her irresponsibility. Maybe Mom repeated it to Dad over dinner – I can't recall. I do know that everyone in my family finally heard it. It became kind of our joke when she'd aggravated anyone. Turn off the television and tell me to do my homework? Jonelle, you have irked me. Go to bed? Irked me to the core. I still wonder if it made her laugh, or if she just grinned and bore it, like the weight of all her stuff.

CHAPTER 4

Fish

My parents split up when we were in that house with terrazzo floors. They wouldn't divorce, officially, for years. Mom couldn't get rid of Dad any easier than she could get rid of a bolt of fabric (chintz, houndstooth.) He and his many infidelities had become part of her stuff, as unwanted as one of T.C.'s fan belts, but he was hers, and therefore, she would manage. Truth be told, the divorce wasn't finalized until years later when my stepmother was ready to marry my dad. That was push coming to shove.

I won't go into blame, shame, or even explanations of the many complicated years of my parents' complicated marriage, or of the many years until the wanted, but unsought, and very uncomplicated divorce. I won't muddy this story of stuff with the story of them. They're another thing entirely, and I honestly believe that, somehow or another, my mom would have stubbornly dragged her stuff around, failed marriage or not.

So this is the part where the tale gets a little hard to tell. At least Tolkien had maps. There are so many characters and locations in the following several years that even David O. Selznick's head would be spinning. (If you're under 25, think "Baz Luhrmann's head would be spinning." It's not quite the same thing, but it'll get you in the neighborhood.) Please bear with me. She's worth it.

So, Mom and Dad split up. It was a time when it appeared that nearly everything was splitting. My mom's sister, Becky, had "split": left for her new matrimonial home. Linda had split, all the way to the other coast. When she finally moved back, she'd gotten a place of her own. My uncle Jerry had split: he left the big house with a friend and two bikes on the back of a VW, and he never came home again. He was everywhere, but mostly in Hawaii by then. My eldest brother, Carl, had split from the family, joining the Air Force and heading off to be taught Arabic somewhere in California.

My other brother, Casey, with just a year left in school, seemed to be splitting as well. He was with my mom and me, then with my dad, then back with us, then living with friends. I always thought he'd graduated and found out only recently that in the clusterfuck that became our lives, he fell a couple of credits short and never got his diploma. Hard to believe, as smart as he is. I'm sure he was spinning, just as I was, only in his own direction.

In the midst of the madness, my mother was pregnant, and in 1979, a baby was born.

She told me she was pregnant sometime in January. I was on the couch, feet in her lap. I'd broken my ankle badly just weeks after our move. When she came home from work at night, she would rub my "good" foot and the toes of the wounded limb as they stuck out, still swollen and discolored, from the cast.

That particular afternoon, she seemed different. Worried. She cleared her throat. It was a sound I knew. It was my mom preparing to speak through her tightening throat and watering eyes about something difficult.

"Sue," she said, and I winced inside.

I never liked being called "Sue." When we were younger, my brothers used to say "Suuuuueeeeyyy!" – like a call for pigs – and I always thought it was mean. I'd never said anything about it. I grinned and bore it. Today was no different because my mom looked really serious. My heart was already racing.

"I'm pregnant," she said.

Her voice was not happy. This was not happy news. I didn't understand. I didn't know how to say that I didn't understand.

I do not know how long it took me to say, "Oh."

"It's just, um," she cleared her throat again, and wiped a tear away. "It's that, um, it's not. Um . . . " The rattle in her voice forced her to clear it again. "The baby isn't your dad's."

Again, eventually, I managed, "Oh."

"I'm going to give the baby up for adoption. It's . . . " Her voice broke. "It's best."

I was no stranger to adoption. While we lived in the big house, for several years my parents had taken in "unwed mothers" through an adoption agency. It helped pay the mortgage and helped the young women conceal what their hometowns could not accept. They were always young, always from towns a couple of hours away, or more. They stayed with us, two at a time sometimes, in one of our bedrooms. They would come just as their bellies began to swell, and stay until their newborn baby was placed into the arms of parents who would love and raise the child, they hoped, in ways they themselves simply could not.

I loved all "the girls" that had stayed with us. They were nice to me. They taught me songs and drew pictures with me, and one, Tracy, had hair that smelled like strawberries. We would walk to the store together, where I would spend the entire visit smelling lotion and cocoa butter and opening every shampoo in the bargain bin, trying to find anything that smelled as good as Tracy's hair.

I was thinking about every single one of the pregnant girls we'd known, and how they'd come and gone, and I looked at the ceiling, my cast, my toes, everything but my mom, as I brushed away tear after tear. I always thought the girls that came to our house had been lonely, so far from home for so many months. I didn't want my mom to be lonely. She was right there, but she seemed lonely already.

She asked me whether I had questions.

"When. . . ?"

"April. Sometime. You know, it's never for sure."

It was so quiet when she asked, "Do you want to know anything else?" that I jumped, just a little. "Do you have other questions?"

I did. I looked at her, but the lump in my throat was too big to let the thousands of them through. I just shook my head "No," lying, so that I wouldn't sob.

One night in April, my mom woke me up out of a deep sleep.

"Susan," she said, touching my shoulder. "I'm going to the hospital."

I was confused. It was the middle of the night, not time for her shift.

"It's time. The baby's coming."

"You're . . . ? You can't drive. You're . . ."

"I'm taking a taxi." She kissed me on the head. "It's okay. Go back to sleep. I'll be fine."

"But . . ."

"I'll be fine. And Linda will come over tomorrow to get you. You can come see me at the hospital. Okay?"

It was not okay. I was definitely not okay with my mom being alone, about to give birth, with no one to hold her hand on the way to the hospital. I thought that night that "I'm taking a taxi" were the saddest words I would ever hear.

"Okay," I said.

The baby girl was born, and after a very uncomfortable hospital visit with Linda, where I tried hard not to cry, and therefore said very little, my mom came home. I never saw the baby.

Even the family I didn't know was, it seemed, splitting.

The only people left in our house were me, my mom, and my uncle Charlie, my mom's youngest brother. I don't even know why he stayed so long, but I was glad he did; he was good at helping me with homework.

After a year and a half in the house with terrazzo floors, as the 1970s were winding down, my mom traded in her gurus and muumuus for self-actualization and EST. (That's Erhardt Seminar Training, as it was known in its later days. It was called "Est," the Latin word for "it is," in its early conception.) Around the time I was completing sixth grade, Mom decided to split entirely and move to Miami to be closer to the nearest EST office – they called them "centers." Charlie split then, too.

Miami is some 257 miles from St. Petersburg. That distance seems like nothing as I write this. I've moved across our continent three times, and will drive – have driven – 257 miles to spend a weekend somewhere many, many times in my life. But at the tender age of 11, my entire universe existed within a 20-mile radius. Miami was a big, scary city, which the local news would lead any child to believe was full of hoodlums, illegal immigrants and danger. (I don't think I even knew what an immigrant was, but if the word "illegal" came in front of it, it had to be bad, according to the innocent and unadulterated mind of an obedient Catholic child.)

I really didn't want to go to Miami. To me, big cities sounded a lot like giant public schools, the kind I'd only heard about, with kids carrying knives and beating each other up over lunch money. Bigger classes, bigger bullies. Less time to get the teacher's attention, and therefore exponentially more difficult to become the teacher's pet. Bigger bullies and no teacher to intervene seemed like certain death to me: a unique, intelligent, and very fat little girl. And the fatter you are, the longer the aisle to your desk is.

(Let this be a lesson to you: Most fat kids *know* they're fat. They don't like being fat. They don't understand, most of them, why they are driven by a deep and compelling need – whether hungry or not – toward the cookies instead of the applesauce. They don't understand the psychology of themselves. They are fat, and they are teased, and they are walking targets for others' cruelty. It does not matter how much they're loved. It does not matter how much they're taught to love themselves. Kids are mean, fat kids get teased, and life isn't easy. The best you can hope for is that when they grow up, they can embrace themselves for who they've become, whatever that looks like.)

So, there was fat, scared me, and there was my mom moving to Miami. Anything seemed better, so I moved in with my dad and Wilma, who would later be my stepmom. I spent a year there. They'd moved into a rental house in the school district that I was already in. Bonus! I wouldn't have to meet any new mean kids, so my tactics for avoiding those whom I already recognized were sure to last me through middle school.

While I was living with my dad, we got along, for the most part. My dad loved me, I knew, even if I wasn't a baseball-playing boy. He did things for me and tried to make sure that I had fun and stayed in line at the same time. He wasn't afraid of raising a girl, and wasn't shy to show it. I got my first period at 12 when I was living with them, and I was so embarrassed. I wasn't sure which one of them to go to first, or how to say the words. (Periods, like sex, were something my family just didn't talk much about.) Once I'd finally managed to tell my stepmother, who handled it perfectly, my father jumped into the car to run to the store for her and get things I might need. He wasn't embarrassed. He didn't mind. He always said something like, "If somebody sees me buying that stuff, it means I either have a wife or a daughter. Either way, if he says something about it, he's probably jealous I have someone to love."

My dad wasn't ashamed of much. Then again, he wasn't raised Catholic. He was raised a Southern Baptist, and his father nearly didn't attend my parent's wedding because his son was marrying a Catholic girl. My grandfather wouldn't have been there, I'm told, had my grandmother not chosen the event to be the one – and perhaps only – time she put her foot down, insisting that her husband be at their son's wedding, regardless of dogma. He must have felt the spirit of righteousness move in her, even feared heavenly retribution, because he did eventually consent to attend.

When I lived with Dad and Wilma, I went to the mall on the bus every Saturday and bought myself a new record album. I financed my habit by getting up early and cleaning up after my dad's weekly Friday night poker game. He paid me 20 bucks a week, which was just a small piece of what he usually won, but it was great income for a 12-year-old. Dad's gambling taught me things, too, like what "scared money" was and why no one should play poker with the rent. That 20 bucks a week taught me a little about responsibility and freedom. Years later, it also helped me to learn why an album by, say, The Beatles or AC/DC might be a better investment than an LP laid down by Rupert Holmes. (Who? Exactly.)

Wilma had already raised three boys herself, so raising a daughter didn't come naturally to her. We had our differences, and she was much more uptight about little things than either of my parents had ever been. I was not to walk around the house, for example, in a nightgown unless I was also wearing a robe over it. But she made it important when I had concerts at school, and she eventually learned how to lighten up and laugh a little. We did okay, until they moved away.

Their departure was supposed to be easy; the transition was to be less than traumatic for me. Dad had the promise of a great opportunity in Washington State, working with a newly constructed nuclear power plant. They needed to move quickly if the work was to be his, so they packed up and left just before the end of my school year. I was going to spend the last few days of school there, in Dad and Wilma's house, with my stepbrothers. One of my best friends lived right behind us, and I was used to taking the bus to school with her. Her mom was always around, or her big brother, so my dad felt confident that there were enough adults to handle one child. Once school was out, I'd go to Aunt Becky's house to spend the summer. At least until Mom came back . . .

After I'd been at Becky's for about a week, I asked to be taken back to Dad and Wilma's place. I still had the key, and my stepbrothers were going to be staying there for the weeks left on the lease, so I hadn't yet taken all of my things. We headed over on a Saturday morning, but no one was home. As we crossed the porch, and I put my key in the door, something smelled fishy. Literally.

The scene inside was homicide. Or, pisces-cide. I never could have imagined it. It was unimaginable.

My stepbrothers, it seemed, had been on a rampage. My family – Mom and my aunts – suspected they drank and did drugs. No one was sure which of my step-siblings was using what, and for a while, my brother, Casey, who had moved away, fell into the fractured family portrait again. He'd been living in Hawaii with Carl, and while there, he had a drug-induced psychedelic experience – or several – that left him deeply unsettled, so he had been "sent home" by Carl to heal under the refuge of our father's roof. Casey was keeping company with Wilma's sons, and together they stirred up trouble, intended or not. Items disappeared. Things got broken. My Dad's class ring had gone missing shortly before he and Wilma moved to Washington.

Things in that house were getting strange, but I never felt unsafe. It had been unsafe, though, for Wilma's goldfish.

There had been about 15 of them in the tank, but Joe and Charlie were the first and the best-loved. They weren't fancy goldfish. They weren't bobble-eyed or beautifully painted with gold and white. They didn't have fantails. They were the plainest, most straightforward, won-in-a-carnival-game-looking goldfish I'd ever seen. But she loved them. She talked to them. They swam to the top when she fed them, and sometimes she'd stick a finger in and pet them. Wilma was a simple country girl and didn't need to grant things unusual or imperial names like I did. My pets, teddy bears, and automobiles, have nearly always been named things like "Andrusa" (pronounced Andrew-sa), "Parsley," "Oliba" (Ollie-bah), "Noodle," and "Dexter." Even my backyard chickens, during my "Rocky Horror Picture Show" phase, had to be named "Magenta" and "Columbia." So fish called "Joe" and "Charlie" seemed boring, even in their names. But Wilma loved them, and she'd had them for several years before the move. They were in a 30-gallon tank, so they grew quite large.

As Becky and I entered the fishy-smelling house, there lay the carnage: Joe, Charlie, and all of their friends, dead all over the living room floor. Stinking fish water flooded the living room rug, so it squished as we stepped in. Gravel had spilled out into a perfectly shaped peak, like the sand in the hourglass that started one of my dad's favorite soap operas. One of the "boys," or perhaps all of them, had decided that there was nowhere better to store a baseball bat than in the front of a fish tank. So they'd bashed it in, let the bat hang there, and left.

I couldn't understand it. Some things can't be explained, but I wanted answers. Wilma's most beloved creatures were dead, and their home – her prized possession – was demolished. The fish had all been left flopping on the floor until they suffocated. Could someone have broken in? How could I possibly be related to someone mean enough to kill Wilma's fish?

When I realized, standing there, that senseless violence was, in fact, the only answer, that the world was not safe (in fact, it was very *un*safe), and that people sometimes hurt things for no reason whatsoever, I began to cry. I didn't stop for months. Okay, I stopped. But I cried. Every day. And I had a lot of horrible dreams about dead fish.

Later that summer, I also suddenly had no home. Mom decided that she didn't want to come back from Miami yet. Dad was already gone. My parents, in their infinite wisdom, gave me – at the tender age of 12 – the opportunity to choose between them. Did I mention that I'm ridiculously loyal? There was no choice I could make.

If Miami was too far, Washington felt light-years away. I couldn't even imagine it. I didn't know the names of the trees that grew there, or what kinds of birds inhabited them. I didn't know the street names, the bus routes, the grocery stores. When would I ever see my friends again? Or my family in Florida? How did people live in Washington State, and why should I want to live there? If I moved to Washington, my mom would forever know that I didn't love her enough to stay. If I moved to Miami, clearly my dad would know that I hadn't loved him enough to go to where he was. Both places, and both concepts, were as foreign as Jupiter, Mars, or Pluto (which at that time was still a planet).

So I stayed there, in St. Pete, and lived with my mom's sister, Linda, for a year, flopping around, eyes wide and stunned-looking, like pre-mortem Joe and Charlie, until my mom decided to be a mother again.

CHAPTER 5

Criminal

My mom's adventures in Miami were brief. She lived there for two years. For about a year, she lived in a house with a roommate – a woman named Gloria. I know that Mom worked a lot, and the rest of her time was filled with volunteering for EST or taking EST seminars. I'm not sure where her stuff was. I visited her once while she lived in the house with Gloria. She had stuff there, but it was shrunken, more specific. Her bedroom was small, with only a twin bed and two dressers, and just one corner filled with stuff. It was work stuff, clothing stuff, stuff to hang on the walls. Somehow, though, I think that even that much stuff was too much for Gloria. Mom moved out, and after she did, I almost never heard Gloria's name again. I think Mom owed her money. I also think Mom had irked her. Irked her to the core.

Mom moved into another house with her two gay best friends, Jim and Tom. They already had stuff, so somehow it seemed like they understood Mom, and her stuff, or at least tolerated it better. Tom had lots and lots of stuff, but his was mostly in the form of 33 RPM vinyl. Jim had lots of stuff, too, but most of his stuff was books. In Jim and Tom's house, I learned that books and records were great stuff, because that kind of stuff could be placed in neat rows on shelves, and it almost appears to have a purpose. You can keep lots and lots of that stuff around, and as long as you keep it neatly, no one thinks you're crazy. You're a collector. Mom had stuff in their house, too, but it was piled in her room. It didn't look as cool as their stuff, although my mom believed every piece of it had a purpose.

At the time, I thought a lot of things about my mom:

I thought she was all wrapped up in something that seemed a lot like a cult.

I thought she didn't really want to be my mom very much anymore.

I thought that she believed Miami was a better place than St. Pete, because when we talked on the phone, she always told me stories about things that had happened there, and those things were nothing that would ever happen in St. Pete.

I thought that Miami was dangerous for her, because she told me about someone trying to rob her of her purse in broad daylight.

I thought she might die before I ever saw her again, because she used to say things like, "I worked 16 hours before I got in the car to drive up here and come see you. I woke up 3 different times as my car was veering into the other traffic lane. Whew!" And she'd laugh, like it was nothing. She'd make plans to fly up to see me, and tell me about how she had slept in the airport terminal the night before. It scared me. At 12, sleeping in public wasn't something that seemed particularly safe, and the only people I'd ever seen do it were usually covered with newspapers and surrounded by pigeons.

I thought she was reckless and daring, like a wild animal loosed for the first time, shaking off years of captivity. She was beautiful, brave, and more than a little crazy. I was always a little afraid that I'd grow up to be like her someday, and that usually didn't feel like a great thing.

My mother's psychology is something that I'll never fully understand. In the early '80s, she loved the EST training and was committed – heart, soul, and pocketbook – to Werner Erhardt and his crew of trainers. The EST training morphed into the "Forum," offered the "Communication Workshop," sprouted like-minded spinoffs like "The Enlivening Weekend," and germinated seminar series with one-word titles about powerful subjects like "Money" and "Sex." (I was young and had been raised by both Southerners and Catholics, so I could not fathom what had become of my mom that she could sit in a room full of 200 or so strangers and discuss things like sex. That was the kind of thing we didn't talk about.) When my mom finally "got it," she wanted *everyone* she knew to "get it," too. She was a powerhouse of "opportunities," transformative lingo, and reasons for people to "get off it." She was "responsible," and had come to see that "there are no accidents," that you choose whether or not to be "a victim." She wanted to "make a difference."

Somehow, her countless hours of volunteerism and months upon months of seminars became a burden of sorts. I recently read about a study that was done about human willpower and self-control. It seems that self-control is, in fact, not an unlimited resource. It is actually more of an exhaustible commodity. So, for example, if a person who loves junk food chooses to eat nothing but whole, healthful food and avoids all "treats," the longer the avoidance behavior is performed, the more likely it becomes that this behavior will "break," self-control will waver or run out, and some unhealthy food will be more appealing than the choice to exercise self-control. I think that's how it went for my mom: She gave and gave and gave. She exercised tremendous self-control, allowing herself little time, money, sleep, or freedom, and instead devoted every waking moment to one cause or another – nursing or EST.

Unsurprisingly, then, in 1981, she began to feel that her life was out of balance again. She was working all the time but never had any money. She didn't seem to correlate this with the numerous expensive seminars she attended, each one bearing the promise to repay itself tenfold if only she employed its principals just so. She was busy all the time, but rarely fulfilled. She was with people all the time, but always felt alone. She grew resentful and began to feel as though her dedication deserved recompense. So one day she stole $2,000.

Did you just re-read that last sentence? It says what it says: She stole $2,000.

SHE STOLE TWO THOUSAND DOLLARS. (Look, I know Bernie Madoff stole more, but this isn't his story, so just take a second: $2,000, right then, was about what she'd earn in a month of 12-hour shifts, 6 days a week – with a double-pay holiday thrown in – nursing in a neonatal ICU. $2,000 was a windfall, striking gold. $2,000 made her feel rich.)

I didn't know when it happened. I was still living with my aunt Linda, riding my bike to school, listening to Cheap Trick and Journey in the carport of my best friend's house, and sweating in Florida's springtime. One day when I got home, there was a box of things that my mom had sent to me. She did that sometimes (to remind me, I thought, that she did still want to be my mother, just not enough to raise me at the moment). It was usually something pretty, like earrings that would tarnish after I wore them for a few months, something creative – a fountain pen and ink or a wax embossing set – a book (she always remembered who I liked to read), or something for me to wear. This time was no different . . . to the untrained eye.

I opened the box, and on top of the tissue paper was a card. I'd always been told that it was rude to open a gift without reading the sentiment first, so I followed my conscience and opened the card. I could tell it wasn't from "The Stack": a collection of greeting, birthday, new baby, anniversary, sympathy, wedding, sympathy-for-the-wedding, all-occasion, and blank-inside cards that my mom had compiled over the years. The Stack was not like "stuff." It was ever-present, but ever-changing. It never got much smaller or larger. The Stack – including size- and color-appropriate envelopes – was generally somewhere between 4.6 and 4.8 inches tall. My mom and I shared the greeting card sickness, and, from the time I could read, we'd spend hours in the Hallmark store. The sales ladies there knew us, I now realize. One of us would get tickled by a card and show the other, who would in turn catch the giggles – and within seconds, the two of us would be uncontrollable.

For instance, on one very memorable spring day, Mom and I were in Hallmark. "Look, Sue," she said, holding out a very plain-looking card, chuckling, her hand in a fist, but over her mouth, like she was trying to not laugh, cry, and pee herself all at once.

I looked at it, expecting something golden, since Mom's body was shaking with suppressed guffaws. The front was a violet background with no words, only a small photograph of a walrus with an Easter Bunny suit drawn onto it.

Inside: "I am the walrus. I am the egg man."

"Pfffftttttttttt! HaHAAAAAA!" I could not contain myself. I hadn't seen it coming.

My eruption gave her permission to continue breaking the silence, and like giddy schoolgirls, every attempt we made to quiet our ruckus only made us laugh more, harder, louder.

"Shhhhhh," I'd whispered, trying to regain control. I have always had a feeling that stationery stores felt a little like libraries, and therefore the use of hushed tones should be observed there.

"Coo-Coo Ca-Choo," Mom said, and burst out laughing again. Breathless, teary-eyed, nearly creating a scene, we leaned on the end of the shelves for support as if we might actually slide to the floor and die of laughter, and then we wiped our tears so that we could read on, until either we'd read every funny card we could find or simply exhausted ourselves.

As familiar as I'd become with The Stack, I didn't have to know the individual cards in it to know when a card came from it. Certain cards were bought for The Stack: Cards she could send anyone, cards she "needed" to keep around, in case she was invited to an emergency baby shower (Congrats?), or had an unannounced visit from a recently married, distant second-cousin (Congrats!). They weren't five-dollar cards. They were "season's ended" cards and sale cards and buy-three-get-two-free cards. The Stack cards were good (we don't give bad cards in my family), but they weren't five-dollar cards. When she sent a goodie box to a family member, they got a blank-inside card from The Stack, usually with a macro-photography image of a flower, or maybe something from the World Wildlife Fund – a fox in the snow, a bear. She sent free or almost-free cards with goodie boxes.

But the card inside the top of the box that day was a five-dollar card. It was jewel-toned and paisley and gold-embossed and had touches of velvet and a golden tassel hanging off the bottom from a cord that kept the paper inside in place. The paper lining the inside of the card was linen, I thought, or silk. It was a blank-inside card, but it was clearly, most definitely, a five-dollar card.

She'd written, "I hope you like these things. I thought they were so pretty, just like you. I love you, Mom." A typical, though always-appreciated, sentiment from her. She was never shy with her love.

Having done my moral duty by completing the reading of the inscription, I pulled back the tissue paper. (This, too, was a bit of an upgrade: usually it was yesterday's news.) Inside was a collection of some of the most beautiful things I'd ever been given: A journal. A set of colored pencils. A box of stationery. A blouse.

The journal was handmade, painstakingly. The thick, fibrous paper inside was all crafted by the same ten digits that had bound those leaves into the form of a book, and mounted it to the cover, which was itself a hand-created spectacle – a tie-dyed firework of color. Something you wouldn't ever, ever doodle in or take phone messages on. I felt I'd graduated. I'd never owned "a journal." Until then, I'd only had a diary with a tiny, ineffective lock – the kind you used to find in every drugstore and five-and-dime. A journal was *more*, bigger, offering possibilities beyond the events of the day. A journal was definitely an important thing to have.

I'm not suggesting that doodling is unimportant. Hunter S. Thompson proves otherwise. I am simply saying that I would never doodle in a journal. At least not then, in my first journal, a very lovely and important book. I stayed up all night once with a friend, thinking and talking about that, and about art and drawing and life – and at some point in the seventh hour of drinking, I finally realized something. It hit me more clearly than things usually do after two bottles of wine: I don't doodle because Mary, my best friend, did in second grade. Okay, we all did. We doodled in library books. We drew things that we didn't understand, things that we were just learning about, things that we thought were funny: boobs, butts, penises. Silly faces. Then one day Mary got caught.

You do *not* get caught doing things when you go to Catholic school. It is a very bad idea. Shame doesn't fade in that place quickly or for long. I was sitting next to Mary when Sister Veranita caught her. I may have even been the one who actually drew the boobs, but Mary got caught, and Sister Veranita publicly shamed her. I could never look her (the nun, not my best friend) in the eye again without sweating. So, no offense to doodlers – chronic, professional, artistic, or otherwise – because I like doodles, I really do. But Sister Veranita said I shouldn't, and, like my mom, I still hear the echo of every superior's reprimand when I fall out of lockstep with their dictates.

In the goodie box, underneath the handmade journal and five-dollar card, was a set of colored pencils. They weren't Crayola – far from it. They were from the kind of stores that I loved to walk through, dreaming: art stores. They were serious colored pencils, the kind that an artist – a *real* artist – would use. Prismacolor. Prismacolor. I said it over and over. The pencils were in a black padded case, and when you flipped the top up and over, it became an easel of sorts, holding the pencils upright so that the artist might view the infinite array of colors before her. It was very impressive, so much so that I left it open, propped up, in my room for weeks. They were an extremely important kind of pencil. (Also, not for doodling.) The funny thing about that is that I kept those pencils nearly forever

– or, should I say, about 30 years – until the case was falling apart, half-melted from a ride in a moving truck through the Mojave in mid-summer, and even then, I salvaged the pencils that remained unglued to the plastic case. They were still very lightly used. I doodle much more than I do serious art, it seems. I will now admit I have even irreverently doodled with the remaining robin's egg blue, coral, and aquamarine pencils.

The stationery set was a thing to behold. It was laser-cut at the top, an intricate design – so intricate that I always had to be extra-careful when lifting a sheet of the paper from the box, lest it tear one of the tiny, tiny strands that composed the design. This was the early '80s, remember – "laser-cut" still meant ultra-cool, progressive, and "You probably can't afford it." I have deliberately reminded you of the era before revealing the nature of the design: a unicorn frolicking in a garden full of flowers (foxglove, bearded iris, freesia.) I'd be embarrassed today, but I was 12, and my laser-cut unicorn stationery *rocked*. The envelopes were thick, nice, felt good against the fingers. I could tell that ink wouldn't smear easily on them. They were almost as fancy as the kind of envelopes that I'd seen in the big books at the Hallmark store – the kind that usually held fancy printed invitations for very important events.

The blouse underneath all of the other gifts was not something she'd made. She didn't sew much at the time; I guessed there was no room to sew in Miami, though she still had, somewhere, her Singer sewing machine. It would resurface later, along with a few bolts of familiar fabric and nearly half of the enormous kaleidoscope of Mom's collected buttons (glass, wooden, Bakelite).

She was a mystery, my mom. I'd be certain some missing item had disappeared, worn out, or been broken in a move when, voila! The corner of it would come poking out of some old suitcase, box, or milk crate somewhere. Better yet were the few occasions when "final notice" for payment of rent on a nearly forgotten storage unit arrived in the mail. Suddenly, a wealth of nearly forgotten possessions would be reclaimed: stacks of our family's favorite board games; cherished souvenirs from trips to Disney World; entire sets of bed linens that I'd spent hours using fabric paint called "liquid embroidery" to decorate with faux cross-stitch; appliances; sewing machines . . .

But Mom hadn't sewn this blouse. It was more than pretty: It was magnificent. Jewel-toned fabric (amethyst, emerald, sapphire), completely unlike anything I'd owned. It was an exotic print – from Marrakech, maybe, or Morocco, or perhaps even Istanbul (that's Constantinople). It was bordered by rows of trim, but it wasn't wavy bric-a-brac; it was soft, thin lines of burgundy satin, alternating with soft, thin lines of velvet in the same shade. It wasn't dressy, fussy, frilly. It was casual and stunningly elegant. It was the nicest thing I'd ever owned that I wouldn't wear to church or a wedding. (Not then, anyway. I'm not terribly familiar with the inside of churches these days, especially when they're filled with congregants, but last I recall, jeans are acceptable in church now, as are flip flops and t-shirts. I'm not saying that's a bad thing. I think it's freaking *great*. I've never much believed in protocol when it comes to talking to the Big Out There. Pray naked, why not? But I'd have been hung out to dry wearing dungarees into our church at the time.)

The blouse was sheer, but just barely, and only at the neckline and sleeves. Nothing inappropriate for a young lady, but something that hinted at the woman I'd someday become. I loved this blouse so much that it was used to within an inch of its life, until the ribbons of satin and velvet wore down and dulled, until the elastic in the puffy sleeves shredded and then broke, until I was a teenager and my bust developed, and it simply would not fit any longer. Even then, it took me a year to throw it away.

So this magical box of trinkets, this "care package," was my introduction to my mother's criminal activity. Sitting in my bedroom in Linda's house, surrounded by the bounty of beautiful things, something in the air was bittersweet. I wasn't sure what to do with such a horde of treasure, and didn't know what I'd done to deserve it. Luxuries didn't come unearned. I wanted to save it, savor it, ration it out to myself in bits, like wartime coffee, so that the wonder I was feeling would last. I felt guilty, and wondered if she'd had any money left for herself and how she'd felt justified spending so much hard-earned money for so many extravagances.

Several months later, I'd learn the truth of what had happened. By then, Mom had had enough of Miami, it seemed, and was ready to strap on the baggage of her youngest (claimed) child again. I'd finished eighth grade living with my aunt Linda, and spent the summer afterwards visiting with my father and stepmother in Washington, where I learned that people in Kennewick were mostly like people in St. Pete. I found out for the first time what "It's a dry heat" means and how sweet a Walla Walla onion is. I found out that I liked Washington State well enough, but it still felt nothing like home. There were hills, not beaches, and the kids were friendly, but they weren't like my friends. We had no history. As September loomed, the decision was made: I'd return to St. Pete and live with my mom again.

We moved into a house that she rented. It was in a neighborhood I didn't know very well, and it was close enough to an industrial development that it felt like we lived in the slums. Our road was paved, but the potholes had been patched so repeatedly that driving on it was no better than on the red brick streets in the northeast (read: nice) section of town.

I can recognize it now as a blue-collar, working-class neighborhood with moderate home security concerns due to surrounding high-traffic streets, but our new house had burglar bars on the windows and felt more like a cage than a house. There were three bedrooms, which was plenty of space for us. I remember her giving me the master bedroom, with my very own bathroom. She said it was because I always took so much time with my hair, so I should just go ahead and take the room with the bathroom attached. I knew it was because she felt guilty for abdicating her duties for two years of my childhood. I didn't want her guilt, but I took the room anyway.

After about a month in our new home, she revealed her life of crime. She sat me down one day and explained why I couldn't have something-or-other that I thought I couldn't live without. She explained that yes, she was doing well with the nursing agency and had made a lot of overtime the week before, but she had some financial commitments that she had to meet right away, so we couldn't be spendthrifts. Then she dropped the bomb.

"You know, sometimes people screw things up, Sue. I screwed up."

Uh-oh, I thought.

"I, um, I made a mistake, and now I'm having to pay some extra money to take care of it."

I looked at her. "I don't get it."

"I, um . . . Well, okay. You know how much work I was doing with EST in Miami, right?"

I nodded. Of course I knew. Wasn't that why she'd left me in the first place?

"Well, you know, they trusted me a lot. Since I started doing the Seminar Leader's program, they'd really been giving me more and more responsibility. I mean, that's a good thing. Or it should have been a good thing. But I messed up and took some money."

Uh-oh.

I thought about my brother Carl's dimes. He'd collected silver dimes when he was young. They'd disappeared during his teenage years, and he was certain mom had sold them. She never copped to it, but we pretty much all knew, if only because she never had much to say about what *had* happened to them.

"I was going to pay EST back," she said. "Well, I think I was."

"What does *that* mean?"

"It sounds crazy, right? I'm not sure exactly what I mean, because I'm not sure exactly what happened. It almost seems like a dream, but it happened. I was leaving the EST Center one night, and someone asked me to drop a deposit at the bank. I told them I would, and I took the pouch. But on the way home, I forgot to stop. I was so tired . . ."

She paused like she wanted me to say something. I couldn't.

"The next morning when I got up, it was like . . . I dunno. It was like something clicked, and I just couldn't take the deposit. I didn't want to. I was tired. I guess, now, I know I was feeling resentful. All of the trainers wear nice shoes and have nice clothes. They take vacations and go places. They travel. I was working all the time but never had any money. I just couldn't get ahead. I can't explain why, Sue, I really can't. I like what I do with EST, but . . . I was spending *so* much time there, and so much money on seminars, and it felt like all I was doing was give, give, giving . . . and for some reason that day I just wanted to take . . . so I took. I didn't take the deposit to the bank. Instead, I kept it. That's not very honest. I stole it. That's the truth. I stole two thousand dollars. At first, I thought I'd just pay it back. I'd come up with the money and tell them that I'd forgotten to take the deposit that night and then found it a few days later, in my car. That wasn't a very good plan, because I'm not sure where I thought the money would come from. I wasn't thinking clearly."

I looked at her. What should I say?

"I'm sorry, Susan. I feel like a really bad mom. I just . . . I wanted to not feel so poor. I wanted nice things. I wanted you to have nice things."

It was quiet for a long time, except for the dog barking next door.

"Did you go to jail?" I asked. Wired for anxiety, I've always feared that bad means worst.

"No. No, I was lucky."

"What happened?"

"After a couple of weeks, they figured out that the deposit hadn't made it to the bank. They started calling me, but I didn't call them back. I skipped my seminars – avoided them for a while. But after a couple more weeks, I just couldn't stand myself. I called the Center and told them what I'd done."

"Did they call the police?"

"No . . . No. I think some of the staff wanted to. We had a long meeting. I talked to them for a long time, and I agreed to pay back the money, and they agreed not to press charges. But I have to pay it all back by the end of next month, so that, on top of moving back and getting the house going, is why money's been tight . . . I'm sorry, Sue. I don't know what else to say. Do you have any questions?"

I could not understand her. I knew what the words meant, but it was all so surreal. My mom, a thief? My mom, a criminal? My mother – the nurse, the caregiver, the kind-hearted champion of aged and newborn alike – an inmate-waiting-to-happen. I had *so* many questions, but they were all stuck just behind that enormous lump in my throat – the one that allowed me only to shake my head "No," so I wouldn't cry and thereby magnify her guilt.

I kept the unicorn stationery almost forever. It was reserved for only the most important letters to the closest friends and most beloved relatives. It was so fancy that it deserved to bear only the most important communications, although each letter mailed was sealed with a kiss and just a little bit of guilt. Okay, more than a little. Until I was rid of all of it, I felt guilty every time I came across its elaborate designs in my desk drawer: stolen paper. Many years later, writing to her from college, I mailed the final laser-cut sheet to my mom. I wondered, as I chose the stationery that day, if she'd remember its genesis in our lives. I told myself that I should not still be punishing her, and knew somehow that I was.

Our three-bedroom housecage had no garage, so the amount of stuff my mom could store was strictly limited to the confines of our four walls. Her bedroom had the ever-present, mysterious "pile," but aside from that, our house was clean, if a bit cluttered, and showed no real signs of an unnatural attachment to things.

We moved in the middle of that school year. I'm pretty sure she couldn't pay the rent. We moved a lot, and I believe that it was often because she'd fallen behind in her obligations. Our next house was small and yellow, with big windows to let in sunlight, and small rooms to keep us close. It was in my school district, only a few blocks away from my then-boyfriend, close to the bus line, and a bike ride to shopping or my friends' houses.

I liked our house. There were only two bedrooms, but there was . . . a garage. And so it began again. It was 1982.

CHAPTER 6

Bounce

While living in the tiny yellow house, our lives took so many fast turns that I was nearly sick from the g-forces. The younger of my two older brothers, Casey, moved in with us for a while. He slept on the enclosed front porch that soon became "his room." He was post-high school, pre-college, post-burnout, pre-massage degree, pre-marriage, post-Hawaiian hallucinogenic adventures, and a little adrift. We got along well enough, even when he brought strangers into the house for the night: friends from Narcotics Anonymous meetings or spiritual gatherings, homeless guys who needed a shower, a pair of German girls with long underarm hair whom he'd met on the beach and offered our living room to in lieu of a hostel. Casey has always been kind, and though some would say "to a fault," I'm not sure there's ever any fault in being kind.

Casey gave me records that he thought were important for me to hear: Frank Zappa's "Yellow Snow," The Moody Blues' "Days of Future Passed," and Pink Floyd's "Animals." I didn't understand all of them at the time, but I do now, mostly. I'll never totally get Zappa, and that's okay; I don't think we're supposed to.

Casey moved out as our brother, Carl, was moving from his most recent home in Seattle back to Florida. A major traffic accident while driving through Texas had left him with a punctured lung and other internal injuries, a wife with a broken leg, broken arm, and broken glasses, and a young stepdaughter with two broken arms. When family needs, family gives – and so, with nowhere to go and recover their health, they all moved in with us. My mom gave up her bedroom and moved into mine. Exactly what every 14-year-old hopes for! With so many people in one tiny house, there's a lot less room for other stuff. So, the stuff went to the garage.

We moved again about a year later, once my siblings had sorted things out and were off to lead their adult lives again. My mom was working in a private home – an "adult congregate living facility" – where the owner took care of ten or twelve "old folks," which is what we always called them. I really don't know how, but we ended up moving all of Mom's stuff, plus the rest of our household, into storage. Then we went to live with the old folks. That was strange. I don't know why we couldn't have a house, or even an apartment, for a while. She'd screwed the proverbial pooch financially again, somehow, I'm sure. What I do know is that we lived with the old folks for a while, three months, I think. I vaguely recall being given a chance to move back in with Aunt Linda at that point, but I was afraid if I lost sight of Mom for too long, she might go spinning out into space and disappear to Miami, or further, again. So I chose the old folks' home.

I didn't have a room there, really. There was a little area off the kitchen – what might at one point have been a small dining room – which wasn't used because the old folks ate on TV tables in their comfortable chairs – that became my roost. It had a pocket door that closed it off from the kitchen, but it was still open – save a few decorative iron bars – to the formal living room at the front of the house. That was mostly okay, too, since the old folks didn't use that room, either. They liked the den and the sunny yard and shady patio out back, or they spent time in their rooms. So the formal living room was only ever used at night, when my mom laid down on the couch there to sleep, usually fully dressed and covered up with only her cardigan sweater.

The only thing I took to the old folks' home, aside from my clothes, shoes, and schoolbooks, was my collection of scarves and a portable typewriter. The typewriter was cooler than any I'd ever seen. It was light and compact, with a red leather cover and a bright red carriage housing. Better than that were the keys: They were all italic, so anything typed on this hot little machine looked extra-fancy, important.

I decorated my roost there by tying my scarves end to end and threading them through the iron bars and tacking them on the ceiling. After a week or so, decoration completed, Mom came in to tell me goodnight one night.

"Sue, I know this has all been . . . Well . . ." She choked up. Mom choked up a lot when she had to find words to talk about hard times. It's probably genetic, the lump in the throat. She sat down on the edge of my bed and started to stroke my hair.

"I just want you to know how much I appreciate how good you're being about everything, all the moving around. It's not easy, I know."

"It's okay," I said, because thought I needed to, not because it was okay.

She looked around the decorated dining nook bedroom. "Your scarves are pretty. I like that polka dotted one. And that one with all the hands on it." She stroked my hair some more. "You're unique, you know? You're a special girl. You adjust so well. I know you've been through a lot, and I'm sorry. It's going to get better."

She told me often that she was sorry, which I hated. When she was sorry, she got sad, and when she was sad, our whole life felt joyless – like a shroud had been pulled over it. Deep sadness would always threaten the beginning of a depression, and depression was the only thing capable of transforming my boisterous, gregarious, fire-sign Aries mother into a quiet, submissive woman I barely recognized.

So I acted happy, stayed in school, kept my grades up, wrote letters to distant relatives and visited those nearby, spent time with friends, was vigorous in my after-school theatrics – hoping that seeing me forge ever-forward would help her be happy. I worked very, very hard not to complain about anything at all and not to ask for, or even allow myself to want, anything beyond the necessary. I'd heard Melissa Manchester's "Don't Cry Out Loud" one too many times and had taken it to heart, sure that my strength mattered more than my sorrow.

I do not use the word "codependent" when I think or speak about us. It would be a crude oversimplification of our relationship. The emotional needs transferred between us were thicker, meaner, and more complex than any pop-psychology term could begin to illustrate.

At night, I sat down at the counter in the kitchen, when the television had to be off – not only because the old folks had gone to bed, but also because I was told to "find something more productive to do" – and I typed. I fancied myself a young S.E. Hinton, and I was certain I'd turn out the next hot teen novel in no time. I soon learned just how many words it took to fill a sheet of onion skin and how long it could take, some nights, to come up with enough words to fill even one. Couple that with having no typing skills, and, well . . . I think I wrote two chapters, and carted them around with me – my own little version of stuff – for a few years thereafter. I was proud of the story, but I outgrew it before I ever finished writing it, and, finally, I burned it.

It was odd living with the old folks. It seemed like every still-life moment of tenderness was framed by the hard realities of aging bodies, fading minds, loneliness, and mortality. When I got home from school each day, and on weekends, I helped my mom with little things. It was like doing my chores, only it was chores for and with old folks. I was particularly fond of one man, to whom I delivered his daily Metamucil, because he always smiled and asked me questions about my day or my schoolwork.

I wasn't sure what to do with some of the residents, though. A couple of them drooled, and I never knew whether to notice and help or to look away so I wouldn't embarrass them. Some of them didn't talk at all. One lady, Marianne, spoke only French, but she spoke less than she cried. She cried a lot.

"Why is Marianne so sad, Mom?" I whispered one day, looking out into the living room from the kitchen's pass-through window.

"I don't know, Sue."

I could tell she was thinking as she peeled carrots. Finally, she said, "Maybe she's sad because she's alone."

"Doesn't she have any family?"

"I think they live very far away."

"Don't they visit?"

"I don't think so. Not often, anyway."

"That's sad." I knew.

I could hear the long swish-swish-swish of the metal vegetable peeler as Mom stripped the carrots of their peels. We were both thinking, lump-in-throat, about our own long distances. Then, Mom did what she so often tried to do – lighten the mood.

"Maybe she's just sad because we make her wear a nightgown."

"Huh?"

"Maybe Marianne's only crying because she doesn't like her nightgown. She tries to take it off all the time."

"She does?" I laughed. A striptease seemed a spirited contrast to her tears.

"Yes. Poor lady. She gets confused, especially at night. Mary – remember, you met her, the dark-haired lady who owns this home? She says that Marianne used to try to take off her clothes at night and wander out of the house."

"Oh, my gosh. Did she ever make it outside?"

"I don't think so. But maybe. Because now she has to be restrained when she sleeps."

"Restrained? Like tied down?"

"Yes."

"But . . ."

"I know. But it's for her own safety."

"All night?"

"Yes."

"No wonder she cries all the time."

"It's hard to be alone," she said, because she knew. "It's hard when nobody speaks your language."

That day, I started counting the weeks until we were supposed to move again.

Our next house was back in our old neighborhood, right next door to the cagehouse. It had windows with bars on them, too, but had big trees in the yard and a big shed out back with a covered patio. It was close enough to my high school that I could walk. And it had room for stuff.

All of my mom's stuff from the garage at the yellow house was moved into the shed at the new house. And slowly, over the next three years, the stuff grew. The stuff slowly took over the shed, then the patio, and finally, a third bedroom and the shelves in the laundry room that are *supposed* to house things like laundry detergent and bleach.

The growth of a mass of things is slow and sometimes invisible. It began innocuously enough, every time. Mom would be visiting a friend, or on her way home from work, or feeding ducks at the lake, when she'd pass a garage sale, and there it would be, calling to her: a bentwood hat rack, just perfect for that nook inside of her sister Becky's door; an antique shelf that was beautiful but needed a little love and would be perfect to replace the shelf in the corner of our living room – which did not really need replacing; an old board game with all the original pieces that she swore she'd put away for her grandchildren, so someday she could show them how that game "was really played"; a lamp in need of a shade and rewiring that would be just perfect in her best friend's living room, so she'd buy it and fix it up for her – "Christmas is just around the corner, you know!"

My mom was sensitive, intuitive, emotional. Voices rose up from things, and she heard them. Treasures from others' pasts called out to her like so many sirens, and she hearkened, bringing home the surviving wreckage from someone else's disaster, saving it as if she could somehow save their world – repair their lives – by keeping whole the things that they once knew.

It didn't seem to matter that money was nearly always an issue: She bought and brought home stuff. Mom had an uncanny incapability with money, an artful dis-ease, a slippery clutch. Somehow it didn't connect in her brain that stopping at a garage sale on the weekend and bringing home $75 worth of stuff – a huge collection of "Life" magazines, antique picture frames, "new" water bowls for the cats, a telephone shaped like lips that she thought I'd want in my room – had anything to do with the fact that paying the rent the following week would be a real struggle. Not having money to pay bills for too many weeks in a row usually led to depression, and depression led to disappearing into her room as often as possible to sleep, or to sit or lie on the bed, staring, while still somehow appearing to function well enough to get up when she had to go to work.

Eventually, the money would be made, somehow, though it wasn't always nursing that kept the bills paid. Mom was never too proud to work hard, glamorless jobs. She cleaned houses, worked at a dry cleaner, sold Shaklee, Amway, and Mary Kay. Even through her depression, she found ways to keep pushing on, and eventually the rent would be paid, and the clouds would lift – and then, some other sunny Sunday afternoon, a garage sale sign would speak her name, and she would go rushing in, to rescue someone else's memories – and find more stuff.

She was still sleeping after a night shift at Children's Hospital ("11:00-to-7:00 NICU always pays best, especially on weekends, and anyway, those babies need so much love") when I answered our door on a Saturday morning to find two policemen standing amidst the fallen leaves on unswept pavement. I couldn't for the life of me figure out what they'd be doing there. I knew I hadn't misbehaved – not in any really bad, police-involvement kind of way – and I knew my mom had finished repaying EST the $2,000 – plus some kind of interest or restitution.

Hell, she was already back *into* EST (Cut here to Michael Corleone's "Just when I thought I was out, they pull me back in" speech), and after she created a strange brew of insistence and boondogglement, she'd gotten me to drink a few sips. So I found myself in the EST training at 14. Truth be told, I intentionally stalled her until I was 14 because I wanted to be in the adult EST training, not the training for kids. I had never liked sitting at the kids' table, so I was certain the kids' training would bore me.

During my first EST training, I "got it." That's what people in EST said when an idea was realized, hit home. Once all the material in the training was assimilated into a new way to view reality, trainees had "gotten it."

I wasn't drunk on the philosophy, but a lot of it made good, logical sense to me, so Mom started taking me to seminars right along with her, which I figured out I could do economically by volunteering on the seminars' logistics teams. I helped set up ballrooms full of chairs to exacting standards, and learned how to letter paragraphs on chalkboards so uniformly that they looked as though they'd been typeset. I ran microphones up and down aisles. I spent countless hours hand-lettering name tags with a calligraphy-style felt pen. I wasn't seeking praise; I just wanted to get it right: perfect, spotless, uniform.

As a reward for my efforts, I got to hang out at these events with a bunch of adults who spoke to me as if I had already learned a little about life and had a mind and an opinion worth hearing. That was much of what I enjoyed, the payoff beyond the philosophy and self-discipline: There were some truths being told, yes, but I really enjoyed being treated like an adult.

Luckily, amidst all of her personal growth, Mom still retained a shred of her Catholic piety. I never ended up in the same seminar as her when they were offering the "Sex" series. I was too young, and I was glad because – as wild as I always wished I was – I had retained much of *my* Catholic piety, and squirmed at the subject of sex in general, but especially around my mom.

So, there I was, with my highly accountable, logistically accurate self on an EST-less Saturday morning, no play rehearsal to go to, my mom sleeping off her night shift – *and there were these two policemen*, asking for my mother. I woke her and told her there were police at the door. She came to the door in her nightgown, went to get dressed after a minute, and told me to call her friend – and Mary Kay sales leader – Carol, that Carol would come take care of things. Then my mother got into the back of the police car and was driven away.

I was terribly confused. I'd heard the police say they needed to place her under arrest, but they didn't handcuff her. Are they supposed to?

I thought she'd finished paying off EST. Hadn't she?

At the same time, I thought this had to be happening because of the money she had stolen in Miami. Didn't it?

I didn't know who to ask anything. Having an unstable parent is very lonely, especially when they are the only parent around. I rarely told people about my mom. I hoped that if I persisted in acting like she was normal, maybe someday she would be. Still, when she went off the rails, I never quite knew who to tell.

The cop car had turned the corner at the end of the block and sped away before I realized it was going to be hard for me to call Carol: Our phone was cut off. Mom hadn't paid the bill yet. ("Yet" was always to be placed at the end of any sentence regarding debts unpaid, I was frequently reminded. Debts would always be paid. Eventually.) So, the phone bill hadn't been paid. Yet. I had Carol's number, and, thank God, I liked her and felt I could call, but I didn't even know where to begin: "Hi, this is Jonelle's daughter. Can you come over? The police just took my mom to jail." I was afraid I'd cry, and then she wouldn't be able to understand me through my sobs; nothing could possibly be worse than having to say something like that *twice*.

I thought about going to my friend Liz's house to make the call. She lived close, maybe five blocks. Liz knew things in our house were a little weird. We walked to school together every day, but one morning when I hadn't made it to her place, she found me sitting on the curb down the block, hacking and wheezing and gasping with bronchitis.

Liz's mom was a little more watchful, and much more cautious, than mine. I don't think Liz was allowed out of the house with a fever, so her mom naturally thought it was strange that I'd been allowed to go to school, sick as I was. My mom didn't know how sick I was. Maybe she'd been depressed and couldn't hear my coughing through the fog. Maybe she'd been manic and overlooked it in her enthusiasm for life. I don't remember. It doesn't matter. I ended up in bed and on antibiotics for days, after Liz walked me back to our house that morning.

But I'd insisted on going. I liked school – *loved* it, usually. And if I stood to miss out on a dissection in marine biology, or an important rehearsal, or an improv class, I'd often stubbornly insist on attending, even if the sky was falling. I wanted to be accountable, dependable, reliable. I liked those words, and lots of adults told me they described me. Unlike many of my friends, I could argue, reason, or downright cry my way into or out of whatever I felt was right, regardless of parental guidance. I'd learned to steamroll my mother, though I wasn't trying to be "bad." I simply thought that, at this point in my life, I had sufficient evidence to suggest that perhaps her guidance wasn't always grounded in anything like reality: evidence like her being taken away by the police on a Saturday morning.

Standing alone in the middle of the living room of our phone-less house, my analysis led me to conclude that Liz could handle the situation and not freak out too badly, but I wasn't sure she'd be home, and I still wasn't sure how to tell her that my mom was on her way to jail. *I* still didn't even know why. Besides, Liz lived five blocks away, and weren't you supposed to *hurry* when someone was in jail? I needed other options.

I stood in our driveway and looked up and down our street. The closest pay phone used to be at the end of the block, but it was gone. So I'd have to walk even further, past Liz's house, to get to a pay phone. I didn't really know anyone on our block. There was a nice couple, though, that lived across the street and a few doors down. They had young kids, and the wife always stayed home. She smiled and waved when she saw me, so I thought she was nice and probably safe enough, and they lived on our street, so they probably understood at least a little bit about life-not-going-quite-the-way-you'd- planned.

When the neighbor answered her door, I told her that our phone was broken, and my mom wasn't home. I asked to use her phone. I called Carol, talking as quietly as I could and trying not to let the nice lady with the kids hear too much of what I was saying. I was so embarrassed that I wasn't really thinking about the fact that she'd probably noticed the cruiser in our driveway, and then had seen it driving past her house with my villainous mother in the back.

After the call, I thanked her and excused myself. She offered me a glass of juice or something, which I turned down, but it didn't matter. She didn't care if I had juice; she just felt sorry for me. I knew it, and walked home looking at the potholes in the asphalt.

Carol came over and made sure I was okay. She offered to let me stay with her. I liked her little studio apartment a lot. It was tiny, with room for a bed, dresser, desk and chair, kitchenette and bathroom. Not too much room for stuff, and a balcony that made me feel like I was a bird in the trees. I could imagine myself living in a place like that. I liked Carol, too, but I declined with my best Garbo: "I vant to be alone."

I did want to be alone. I had everything I needed by way of food, and I was already becoming a good cook. I had books, records, a television, and myriad ways to entertain myself on top of the homework I had to do and the lines I needed to learn for a scene I was working on for drama class.

I wanted the silence and control that I felt when I was alone. I did not want to talk. I did not want to explain what I did not understand. I did not want someone else to try to explain my own mother to me. I knew, no matter what they said, they did not really understand at all either. I did not want to be around friends and have to lie, saying that nothing was wrong. I did not want their pity. I did not want anyone to look at me when I was not looking. I did not want the world to have more ammunition against me.

It seemed like Carol just got it; I didn't have to explain a lot. She gave me money in case I needed it. She wanted to be sure I was fine without a phone. She told me she'd stop by on Sunday, just to check on me.

Late Saturday afternoon, when the sun was about to set, Liz knocked at my front door. She'd tried to call, but the phone was out, so she and her brother-in-law had driven by, coming home from the store, and had seen the lights on. She figured my mom was at work and wanted to know if I could spend the night. We'd often sit in her room and listen to the soundtracks from "Grease" and "The Rocky Horror Picture Show," and pretend that nothing mattered but boys, clothes, and nail polish.

I looked at Liz's brother-in-law in the car, and tried to imagine riding the few blocks to her house making small talk. The thought exhausted me, so I told her I had to stay home. She asked about the phone being out, and I told her mom had "forgotten" to pay the bill.

She rolled her eyes and said, "Ugh. Sorry," giving me the half-frown that always told me when she knew there was more to something than what I was saying. There was a beep from the waiting car, so I told her we'd talk at school on Monday, and they left. I laid on the living room floor all that night in front of the stereo, playing the records I'd gotten for Christmas over and over, wanting to memorize every word, to name everything, so I could understand.

On Monday, Carol "sprang" my mom, and I learned that Mom had been carted away because of a bad check. She had needed tires a few months before and had written a large check to a local business for four new ones – a binge for her, the retread queen. The check bounced, and bounced, and bounced – jai-alai fast and wicked, just as all-over-the place as her money and her mind.

She ignored calls and letters for months, while she was still giving me extra lunch money and money for the movies. Paying the rent. Putting gas in the car. And – FORFUCKSSAKE! – going to garage sales to drag home more really, really cool stuff that would someday, despite her wishes and her best intentions, become nothing but old crap – and *spending money on it*, while her signature betrayed her all over town. She was dodging the path of the speeding check, which was by now careening off all of the phone numbers and references she'd given to the bank when she opened her account. So, as they eventually do when the shit catches up with you, the cops came.

Maybe this is *precisely* why I was, still am, and will always be a bit on the timid side, afraid to knowingly break any rule in any way at all, as if I'd swallowed sanctity whole. I've been taught the same lesson time and time again: Do wrong and rest assured, you'll be found out – whether by Sister Veranita or the police.

I loved my mom almost as much as I was embarrassed by her. She always tried so hard to get it right – when she wasn't ignoring whatever "it" was. She was a kind, funny, wounded soul. Who loved stuff. Strike that: Who was compelled to carry the world's stuff everywhere she went.

CHAPTER 7

Toyota

By the time I graduated from high school, it was clear that if I was going to continue a relationship with my mom, I'd have to also maintain a relationship with her stuff. It had somehow become her final child.

I'd tried, once, to discard a jigsaw puzzle that I knew for a fact was missing dozens of pieces, because I saw them fall out of the box and into a city street during a move. She saw it in the garbage can and yelled at me, half in anger, half in disappointment: "Dammit, Susan! I was going to use that!"

"The puzzle?"

"Yes!"

"But —"

"Don't be so sure of yourself!"

"It was only half-there!"

"I know that!"

"But you were going to use it?!"

"Yes!"

"That doesn't even make sense!"

"You don't know! I was going to use it for a picture frame. It's this really neat idea I saw, where you take a plain old picture frame and glue puzzle pieces around it. Dammit!" The anger in her voice waned, but the disappointment did not. "I was going to make one for Sarah, for a picture from her trip to Paris!"

Of course she was. She wasn't lying. She wasn't exaggerating in retaliation for my carelessness. She really had a purpose for her things. Every. Single. One.

Standing there, looking at her, I felt like I'd failed first grade. She looked at me like there was no way I could *not* have known that there was a purpose for half of a jigsaw puzzle. Hadn't she taught me anything?

She had "saved" a Dutch oven missing the lid and both handles that I threw in the garbage – because it had belonged to her friend John, who once served her rice and peas out of it, but John had gotten new pots and pans, so she was going to use it to grow sweet peas.

I caught hell once for throwing away a broken back scratcher – because it had been used by Dr. Mishra, Mom's guru, once during a weekend meditation retreat, and when it later broke, she'd decided she would someday disassemble it and use the round wooden beads to make a necklace for her friend Bonnie, since Bonnie was a massage therapist.

Such scenes repeated themselves with various things over the years until I grew into grim, if temporary, acceptance.

Mom had made it clear: Her stuff was of value. It was not to be scoffed at, treated carelessly, or discarded. Her things all had a remembered place of origin and an intended recipient or use. I could not request that the stuff be diminished in size. I could not suggest that it be sorted through. I could not insist that it be done away with, and I dared not remind her that she'd sometimes done away with people easier than she'd done away with things.

We moved, several months after my graduation, into yet another house – perhaps the most spacious place we'd lived since my parents sold the big house with the sewing room. For once, instead of being in a hurry to move because a lease had run out, or a landlord was fed up with Mom's late rent, time was on our side. We had time to wait, to read the classifieds for weeks, and we drove around in all of our favorite parts of town, looking for a home that we really wanted at a price she could still afford. She believed, then, that she would be able to afford a little more now that I was working and taking care of my own gas, car insurance, and clothing. Once we moved, I started giving her $200 a month, too, and she took it, though she always said she didn't want it.

Our new place had only two bedrooms, but it had a big living room, a dining room equally as large, a den with a fireplace, and a laundry/storage room that could have easily doubled as still another spacious room. The smallish kitchen was comfortable, there was a wide, fenced backyard, and every room had lots of windows and no burglar bars. There was no A/C, the place wasn't fancy, and it was again on busy 16th Street (which helped keep the rent low), but it felt nice to me. It felt big – almost too big for the two of us – but definitely big enough for her stuff.

The moving was intense, insane. My mom, it seemed, had developed a thing against renting trucks to move. Instead, over the years, she'd convinced herself that anything – or nearly anything – could be moved in the backseat, trunk, or on top of whatever old tank of an automobile she owned. At the time, it was a 1969 Buick Wildcat. No mattress or box spring was too large, no bookshelf too unmanageable, to somehow be moved with that car. This, as you can imagine, resulted in dozens upon dozens of trips back and forth from the old house to the new. It took days. Days upon days.

Carrying her stuff into our new house, I'd simply put it where I knew it belonged: in the oversized laundry/storage/soon-to-be stuff room. I didn't need to ask anymore. Frankly, there was no point in discussing it. So I moved, and moved, and moved her stuff. I'd notice from load to load that certain items had gotten damaged, maybe a chipped spot on an old butter churn or a crack in the pane of glass over a lithograph. I saw the gradual decay of possessions, the way the once-immaculate Kewpie doll was now faded by the sun and stained from a drip in the rusty metal roof over the shed at the last house. I saw the boxes of board games defaced and collapsed by time and age. I noticed how all of these things had slowly become of no value at all. And I saw how she clung to them nonetheless.

The reasons for her trouble were, really, as hard to define as our own existence – created by need and desire and love and confusion and mixed motives and blurred emotions. She filled holes in her heart with stuff. She expressed love with stuff. She insulated with stuff. Stuff was protection, and money was just a hassle. But knowing *why* she couldn't balance a checkbook or keep her bills paid – all of them, for one full year without having a service disconnection from one utility or another – didn't change the reality.

We lived in that house for nearly two years together. The older I got, the clearer it became that my mom's ability, and willingness, to deduce logical outcomes from the facts at hand was impaired. She was truly penny wise, pound foolish.

Prime example: Thanksgiving, 1988. I'd finished my Associate's degree on my own dime and was accepted to Florida State University for my Bachelor's in Theatre. I was starting during winter semester, in January, so every major event was now sentimental, being celebrated as "the last" of that kind of event before I would move out of my mom's house and head six hours north to Tallahassee.

During this "last Thanksgiving at home" dinner with my mom and a couple of friends, Mom was eating cranberry sauce, but not the kind we usually had. For years, she'd bought jellied cranberry sauce, which is pureed smooth, not chunky. That year, the cranberry sauce was full of whole berries. Mom stopped, mid-mouthful, and put down her fork. She looked disgusted as she continued to chew until she could finally force a swallow.

She bowed her head, shaking it slowly from left to right. "I hate this cranberry sauce. I've always hated this kind of cranberry sauce," she said, like a kid about broccoli.

Confused, I asked, "So why did you buy it?"

She looked up, the absurdity of it all striking her for the first time, and began to chuckle as she managed to get out the words, "Because it was on sale," before the table erupted into fits of laughter.

A few days later, I came home from work, just after sunset, and flipped on the lamp inside the front door, but it didn't come on. The house was the kind of silent that only comes when there's no power. I knew better than to wonder if the whole neighborhood was out. Rest assured, it wasn't. I knew not to open the fridge; things would stay cold overnight if we kept it closed. From the old ship-shaped mantel clock on the dining room buffet, I could tell they'd shut the power off just before five. We must've been the last work order for the day.

I was pissed because I had money, and if she'd told me the bill was due, or late, or big, or anything at all, I'd have paid it gladly. But Mom didn't talk about problems, usually, until they'd gotten too big to avoid. So here we were, in the dark.

No worries, though, I thought. By this age, I'd become a pro at coping with utility shutoffs and doing quick triage of my needs. We had a gas water heater, so I could shower before work the next day, which was hugely important to me. I'd have to pin my hair up wet. They'd live with it.

That night, after I'd administered an ample dose of the cold shoulder to her, Mom and I stood in the candlelit kitchen, silently eating corn and pinto beans out of cans. We spooned them up with a few saltine crackers, which was what we had that didn't require opening the refrigerator or cooking on our electric stove. As we chewed kernels and beans, Mom commented, "Maybe we should get a gas stove."

I looked up, wanting to say, "Maybe we should just pay the fucking electric bill." She knew I wanted to say it, which made what she'd said absurd. And then funny. And then hysterical. We laughed until tears ran down our faces. We laughed so hard that we had to stop eating for fear of choking to death. We laughed so hard that my sides still hurt when I woke up and took my thank-God-it-was-hot shower the next day.

Since her return from the far-off Miami, and through my increasing maturity, we'd grown close again. Too close. Like scar tissue, we'd laid down assurance after assurance of our love and familial bonds, promising to cling tight forevermore. We had come to rely on one another for everything, two survivors adrift. She'd transcended motherhood and become a friend to me, a choice perhaps as inappropriate as her choice to move to Miami had been. But so it was.

In the two years that I lived at home after high school, I felt in some ways she was re-experiencing her youth. While I worked on my AA degree, I had a steady job working retail. Money was less of a problem that it had been for a long time. I had my own car, so I was not confined. I went alone to visit friends who had moved after high school and were living in Miami, in Orlando. I grew more and more restless, and by October 1988, my looming departure for Florida State University was doom rolling in on a thundercloud over my mom.

I'd read college brochures by the dozens and had hoped for a transfer to Pepperdine, or University of California at Davis, or NYU, but there was no way I'd ever be able to afford out-of-state tuition. Florida State was ranked high for theatre programs at state schools. I was paying for all of my own education and was still too young and passionate to consider more practical degrees. Mom questioned my choice, once, but – without yelling – I roared my leonine roar and said that she should be proud that I was putting myself through college at all, that Becky was the only other person in our family to have managed it thus far, that I had dreams – how dare she tread on them? Just like when I was a teenager with bronchitis, I would not be stopped unless nature itself stopped me.

On the day I moved away, as I hit the clutch and let my tiny car roll down the driveway, I prayed it would make it all the way to Tallahassee and was glad I hadn't decided to go to school any further away.

During my first semester at Florida State, on one of my regular weekly calls home, Mom said that she just didn't need as much space anymore, so she was moving again. I expected her to ask me for help during spring break, but she moved before that. I knew she wanted to spend less money for rent, and she'd found a place – literally across the street – that was owned by someone we knew. Of course, this made it easier to move her things; several dozen trips across the street would have been easier than several dozen trips a few miles away, though I'm still not certain how she did it all.

She often had trouble telling the whole story because there was usually something she was embarrassed by, ashamed about, or felt guilty for. She still carried heavy Catholic guilt, even after years away from the Church. Her bipolar disorder, still undiagnosed, came with a great deal of anxiety, and it was magnified by echoes of the words "stupid girl" from her childhood, whispered by men with cold hearts as they fumbled through her innocence, wrecking it with their calloused hands.

"Be still. Shhh. Be quiet. Stupid girl. You'll wake the others."

Her mother's various boyfriends had planted, very early, the idea that she was a less-than, that she was foolish, and that she definitely should not talk, especially not when things felt wrong. In fact, the more wrong they felt, the less, somehow, she was supposed to talk about them. Self-actualization never made that much easier for her.

I wondered that spring if something had gone wrong during her last move.

"We're almost done!" she'd said, when I called her one evening.

"Done?"

"Moving!"

"Oh. . ." I paused. It was the middle of the month. My mom never moved in the middle of the month. As long as I could remember all of our leases started on the first of the month. "Well, good!" I didn't quite know what to say. She hadn't mentioned packing the last times we'd spoken. "Who helped you? Casey? You didn't do it all by yourself, did you?"

"By myself? No!" Her voice brightened, like either she'd just witnessed a miracle, or she was lying.

"Did Casey help you?"

"Yes. Some. With the big stuff. And he'll be back tomorrow."

I knew what this likely meant: He'd been there and helped her move a good part of the day, and then knocked off mid-afternoon, when the heat is at its worst. He'd told Mom to take the afternoon to get some rest, and they'd do more the next day. Mom, though, was likely too manic to mind that advice, and had probably continued moving her own things, box by bag by box, into and out of the car, to the house across the street.

"You sound tired, Mom," I said, trying to get her to talk.

"It's a lot of work." I could hear her breathing hard still, like she'd been doing heavy lifting when I called. I heard the clink of ice cubes around a glass of water as she paused, drinking. "Boy!" she said, catching her breath. "I've got a lot of stuff!"

"Yes, you do."

"I was hoping to go through a lot of it before I moved, but there just wasn't time. I'll get to it as I unpack, I guess."

Unpack? I marveled at her word choice. There were piles of things that had never been packed in the first place. Just moved, place to place, pile to pile. Unpack? There were boxes that she'd not seen the bottom of for decades. There were treasures purchased for six Christmases (two moves) ago that had been sought for, high and low, waiting still to be unpacked.

I tried to still my judgment and anxiety about how all of this moving was working, exactly, without me. It was like Mom was preparing for a performing magic show, but I didn't like the backstage setup. Shrinking her stuff was a grand illusion and she was about to try to extract a 1,600 square-foot rabbit from a 1,000 square-foot hat, but in reverse. I worried about her ability to pull it off.

"Mom," I said, "I would have helped if you waited 'til spring break."

"I know! But now you don't have to! Now you can come home and relax and enjoy break. We can have fun!"

Her voice betrayed something. A concealment that made her ashamed. She had enormous bookshelves. How had she gotten them across the street? On top of the car? What had happened to the table that broke? Did it slide off the car in the middle of the road, as I suspected a few weeks later when I saw the telltale stripes still on the pavement? Was that what she was hiding? Maybe apology was the whole motive, a desire to get it all done, so I wouldn't be forced to move her again, to continue on as a pack horse. Maybe it was the opposite, and she was still punishing me – just a little – for moving away, by not telling me the stories about the move.

Every move has some, and she knew I loved her stories.

What I'm certain of is that in January 1989, I left for Tallahassee, and when I came home for spring break, we lived across the street.

My mom's new home was even smaller than the tiny yellow house we'd lived in during my freshman year of high school. It had two bedrooms and only one bathroom with a sink that seemed to be several inches too short. The living room bled into the dining room, which sat off of a narrow kitchen. There was a sunroom in the front that was big enough for a couple of chairs but not much else. At least, that's how most of us would have seen Mom's new place. How many cubic feet of stuff it could hold was still undetermined but would soon be tested.

There was a spare bedroom for me, though it was never really "my" room. I'd sleep there during that spring break and two to follow. I'd visit during the summer but would never stay long. Taking summer courses afforded me the freedom to stay in Tallahassee and also to perform in, stage manage, and direct summer repertory shows, which I loved, with my friends, of whom there were many. I was becoming myself, in a more profound way than I ever had while under parental direction. I was learning what I liked, where I stood as an adult, and how to tolerate others, as well as developing a keen sense of the things up with which I would not put. I was growing up, and out, and away from her. No matter how proud she felt, each month that passed was a reminder that we were one month further away from the past, when I was her little girl, and it seemed to somehow make her older – older than she was. I suppose, in hindsight, that's to be expected. Her empty nest led to more bouts of depression, and depression makes us feel every day of our years.

By the time I graduated from college in the spring of 1991, I knew that I never wanted to move home again. I also knew that I had to, at least for a while. All of the caution bred into me – as a Catholic child, a chicken, and a girl in a patriarchal society – had made me a timid adventurist. I wanted to fly, but not very high. I wanted to roost elsewhere, but not so far that I might not return in an instant of weakness or fear. My mother's vacillating moods were reflected in my flesh as an inability to feel entirely at rest, anywhere.

I laugh about this now: What had I not endured at that point? How was the world going to take me down in any way that it hadn't already attempted? What could I not figure out, engineer a way through or around? What could possibly be *less* stable than not being sure whether the power – or lights, water, phone – pick your utility – would be on when you got home?

I spent that summer after college in St. Pete, deciding where to go next, how far would be the right distance; reminiscing about my childhood and raising hell with high school friends; staying *away* from home as much as I stayed *at* home, because it had become claustrophobic and crowded. The piles had grown while I was away and had invaded every room of the small house.

I moved to Atlanta that fall. It was the right time, right place for me. I had friends there, and someone with whom I could share an apartment. It was a big enough city that with just a little luck, I could surely find employment, even with only a degree in theatre on my CV.

Atlanta was a big city, at least compared to where I'd spent most of my time. Interstates 75/85 seemed to be about 12 lanes wide after they converged, even though it was only 8 lanes at the time. I'd heard horror stories about getting lost on Interstate 285, known as "The Perimeter," and driving around and around Atlanta, stuck in purgatory on the way home from work. Traffic seemed inevitable, and the little car I'd been beating around in – a 1972 Honda Civic, bought cheap from my friend Lawrence after my little Plymouth's engine caught on fire in a turn lane during rush hour – wasn't going to last much longer. It was pushing 230,000 miles. I was out of college and believed I needed to take life "seriously." I needed a decent car.

In the early-1990s, the market was filled with Geo Metros and LeCars. I had no idea whether I could afford even an inexpensive model, since I had no idea what kind of work I'd find or how much my rent was going to be. After sitting down with a couple of finance managers, I'd nearly talked myself out of buying a vehicle altogether. But how would I get around Atlanta?

My mom came forward with an offer, a generous graduation gift that I'd never anticipated.

"Sue," she said one morning, as she watched me look at the auto advertisements in the St. Pete Times, "you know, I can help you with a car. I mean, I'd like to."

I looked up from the paper, over my glasses, and joked, "Whachu talkin' 'bout, Willis?"

"I know you want a new car, and it makes sense for you to have one."

"Yeah, Mom, I know."

"So we should go find one for you."

"With what, all of our good looks?"

Mom frowned.

"Mom." I put the paper down. "Mom. C'mon. I don't even have an address where I'll be living in Atlanta yet. I sure don't have a job – "

"Well, you *do* have an address. Don't be so dramatic."

I frowned. I hated being told not to be dramatic, because half of the time – like when she was being arrested, or told me she had fallen asleep at the wheel briefly – I wanted to yell at her, "This situation is *actually dramatic*! I'm not fabricating drama here!" But I tried really, really hard not to raise my voice at my mom.

First and foremost, we really didn't yell much in our house. Ever. We argued like mad sometimes, and cried hot tears doing it, but not usually while yelling. More than that, though, I didn't like to yell at her because of respect. She had raised me (mostly), after all. She was, as my dad used to say, "right, wrong, or indifferent," my mother. One did not disrespect one's parents; I'd been taught it over and over.

"You know you have an address," she continued. "You're living with Lawrence when you get there."

She was right. I had a temporary address until my friend and I found a bigger place to share, closer to town than Doraville - which was a long haul.

"It'll be fine," she tried to reassure me.

This was contrary to what she'd said when I told her I had resolved to move. That erupted into an argument when she'd said I had no car, no job, and no practical skills, railing at me for not even having a typing speed that could get me employment as a secretary. She'd reminded me that retail jobs required nighttime hours, and I hoped to do theatre at night. I'd told her I'd wait tables if I had to, and then she'd said the cruelest words I'd ever heard from her – words I'd never forget: "Nobody wants a fat waitress." My life raft had deflated with one loud pop. I'd begun to question my decisions.

"You'll find a job," she said now, pulling me back from the memory.

"Will I?"

"Of course. You're so bright."

"And so fat." I looked at her, reminding her of the fight.

She looked down. Then she sat down, uncomfortably, on the edge of her armchair. "I'm sorry. I'm sorry I said that last week. I . . . I've thought about it but didn't want to bring it up again. I shouldn't have said it."

Silence, and the room became wobbly-looking from the tears gathering in my eyes.

"Sue. You're very bright. Like you said, you can find temp work, at least to start. Lawrence will help you. And I'm sorry for what I said. You're so pretty. You always have been. You're just so . . . You're so heavy."

I looked across the living room at the gauze around the open ulcer on her ankle. I considered all of the ways that I wanted to bite back, even if her words were true. My mind screamed, "So are you!" and "Runs in the family!" and "I learned from the master!"

But I said nothing.

Nothing except, "I know."

More quiet.

"I know, I am too, Sue."

Great. Now *she* had said what I wanted to say, but I was feeling guilty. Like the words had come from my mouth.

She went on. "I know somehow you . . . I taught you bad habits. And our family – We don't always handle things the best ways, you know? Like, maybe the weight is all the other stuff. You know – we eat when we're upset . . ."

"I know, Mom. Upset. And happy. And angry. And grieving. And celebrating. And bereft, elated, conflicted, confused, hopeful, anxious, bullied, and praised, we eat. I know this."

I knew the psychology of addiction, and I was as embarrassed by talking about it as I was angry that she felt I needed to. It would take me a lot more years to realize that I was angry, too, because I still saw her as the root of all my own shortcomings.

"But, Sue, what I'm saying is, I'm dramatic, too, I guess. I shouldn't have said what I said. You'll find work. People will judge you, and you probably will never be a waitress or stewardess at your weight. But there are lots of heavy people in this world, working. You'll find work. You're bright. You'll be fine."

"Yeah." I looked at the newspaper in my lap.

"Look," she said. "My rent here is so inexpensive. Joan made me a really good deal. So I can help buy you a car."

"But, Mom, your credit . . ." She and my dad had destroyed their credit early in their marriage by raising too many children all at once. I still remembered the voice of the women from Sears Credit and MasterCard who used to call our big house when I was young, and how my mom and dad would ask us to just say they weren't home.

"I know, I don't have any credit. It's been so long, I don't even think it's bad anymore. I just don't have any. But look at that paper, Susan. There are deals all over the place right now for recent college grads."

"I don't have any credit either."

"But that's the point! This is how you build it."

"I dunno . . ."

"You've worked so hard, Sue. You should be proud. You deserve it, and it's a lot better to have a good car if you move away."

"*When* I move away," I corrected her.

"*When* you move away."

I was uneasy. Committing to debts made me squirm, and committing to this much debt was making my palms sweat.

"What if I don't get work right away?"

"I'll make the payments, silly! That's the point. You get the financing for the car, and I'll make the payments for you. Once you have a job and get settled, you can save your extra money, and I'll keep paying for the car."

"Mom, it's a lot – "

"A lot of parents buy their children cars for graduation presents."

"Yes, a lot of doctors and lawyers."

"Sue, it'll be fine."

So there in that moment, and later, in the sales office of a Toyota dealership, I sealed the fate of my future conveyance. Against all of my best judgment, against every neuron firing "No!" signals, against my years of expertise and training in the capriciousness of my mother's promises, I bought a car.

It seemed to have been an effort for her to scrape together the $500 we put down on the car, not to mention the car insurance premium, which I insisted I would take over as soon as I had work. Still, I was excited about the biggest purchase I'd ever made, and I loved my new blue Toyota. It wasn't terribly sporty, but it felt safe and sturdy and like I could drive it for the next ten years, if not longer. It felt like I could get anywhere in it, and I was thrilled with the freedom. "Toyota – Oh, what a feeling!"

Within a month of my move, I'd found a duplex apartment in Atlanta's Virginia-Highland neighborhood with my friend Lawrence. By six months in, I'd found work, albeit as a temp. I'd found a theatre home, stage managing a play at one of the up-and-coming venues in town. I'd developed friendships, been accepted into an internship, taken a newfound interest in my health and weight, and was well on my way to feeling like our family's private asylum had produced a relatively normal, functional adult. A kind of deus ex machina.

And then the phone rang.

It was a weekday, and it was very, very early. I had just gotten up and staggered to the bathroom as I saw Lawrence stagger out of his bedroom. Our downstairs neighbor must've been awaiting the creak of our footsteps, because the phone rang just after we began to move about.

Lawrence answered. I could hear him say, "Oh, hi . . . No, it's okay," and then "Yeah" and "No" a couple of times through the bathroom door, as I peed and wiped the crust from the corner of one eye and wondered what could possibly be urgent enough for someone to call this early. When I opened the bathroom door, he said, "Hold on. I'll check," and placed his hand over the phone.

"You didn't lend anyone your car last night, did you?"

"Huh?"

"You didn't give anyone your keys?"

"No."

"Um. Hm. Okay. You sure?"

"Yeah. What? I mean, why? Who is it?"

"It's Robin, downstairs."

"Okay . . ." Things were beginning to happen in my brain. Bad things.

Lawrence spoke into the phone again. "No, no, she didn't. No, that's okay. Thank you. Thanks for calling, Robin. No, don't worry. It's okay."

By the time he'd hung up the phone, I was shaking. I was shaking so badly I could barely stand. I was shaking uncontrollably from my fingertips to my toes. I had walked back through our kitchen, opened the door, and stared down at the empty parking space that had, the night before, been occupied by my vehicle. Before I even made a phone call to verify, I knew exactly what had happened.

My car had been repossessed.

Remember what I said about being loyal? I was – perhaps still am – foolishly so. I have always defended the good name of my family, my friends, and my closest confidantes with a lion's pride. To suggest that any of my compatriots are cheats, liars, or thieves is as good as insulting me personally. So even once proven a thief (HELLO, TWO THOUSAND DOLLARS!), I could not accept weakness as a part of my mother's true nature. I could not accept that she would, for any reason, *blatantly* lie to me.

There had been phone calls, you see. Several. From the finance company, and a skip tracer, who called himself "Investigator Jackson." And each call to me would in turn necessitate a call from me to my mom, in which she would tell me the bill had just been paid.

"Are you sure?"

"Yes, I'm sure, Susan. I just got home from taking a payment."

"One payment or two?"

"What?"

"Did you send one payment or two?"

"Well, I only sent one money order. . ."

"But for two months, right, Mom? He said we had to pay the two months that it's behind."

"Right. Yes. No, I know. I took one money order, but it was for both months."

"You took it? You mean you mailed it?"

"Yes. I went to the post office to mail it. Well, to get the money order, too."

"Okay."

"I'm sorry, Sue."

"Why? It's okay if you mailed it. But do they know you mailed it? Did you call them? Do you have the money order number?"

"It's out in the car. But I'll call them and give it to them as soon as we hang up."

"Okay. Mom, if . . ."

"What?"

"Well, I mean – if I need to just find another job . . . I mean . . . If I have to work two jobs for a while, I have to. It's – "

"Not necessary. It's not necessary, Sue. It'll be fine."

It wasn't fine, because my phone kept ringing. I'd called Mom back, and she'd told me that she'd put the money order in the envelope the week prior, but forgot to actually drop it into the mail. When the phone rang again, I called her again. Every time they called me, I called her. Every time she had an excuse, and a remedy already in hand. Each and every time – every single time – I believed her. I believed her because she was my mother and because every part of my monkey brain told me I wanted to believe her.

And then my car disappeared.

Lawrence told me later that he had never seen me – perhaps had never seen *anyone* – as brutally angry as I was that morning when I realized that my car was gone.

The phone call to my mom was short. The phone rang and rang, until her machine picked up.

"Mom, it's me. Mom? Wake up. It's me."

It was early, so I hung up and called again, and she answered on the third ring, sleep in her voice.

"Hello?"

"It's me."

"Hi, sweetie . . ." She waited for me to tell her why I was calling so early.

Silence.

"Sue?"

"Yes."

"You okay?"

Silence.

"Sue?"

"No."

Silence.

I continued, "No, I am not okay. I am, right now, most definitely not okay. My car is gone, Mom."

"What happened?" she asked.

I wanted to scream.

"Have you been lying to me, Mom?" I asked.

Silence.

"Have you been lying to me!?" The choking tightness started in my throat, but not before I got out, "My car, Mom? My goddamned car . . .?"

Finally, after a long pause, she said, "I'm sorry."

"You're *sorry*?!" My voice cracked. "You're sorry!? You have no idea. You have no idea how sorry you are. You have no idea how sorry *I* am for believing you." My hands were shaking so badly I could barely hold the phone. "I love you, Mom. I really, really do. But I am so angry. I am so angry. Iamsoangry – Iamsoangry that I really, reallyreallyreallyreally can. Not. Talk. To. You. Any. More. I do not know for how long. Maybe ever."

I sobbed when she said she was sorry one last time.

I said, "So am I."

And I hung up.

I did not call her for weeks. When I finally did, our conversations were cold, strained. Our talks, which had once lasted for hours, now rarely spanned ten minutes. I'd inquire about her health, and she mine, and we'd talk a few minutes about the rest of the family. It was like talking to a second cousin, twice removed. I felt I barely knew her. I did not open my heart – my trust – again to her for months, maybe even years.

I don't recall now what eventually broke down my resistance and sent me reeling toward her love and friendship, though I know that, at the time, I felt so broken that only my mother could repair me. Even then, I'm sure that I still resented needing her care.

Luckily, we grow up and move on. It's a blessing that we are not cursed with being our parents' children for as long as they would have us be. Only by shoveling myself out of the stuff did I avoid being buried by it.

CHAPTER 8

Piss Chocolate

I lived in Atlanta for six years. I only went back to St. Pete twice in that time, and both times I stayed with my aunt Linda. Mom would make excuses about not having cleaned the house, not having done laundry, and therefore not having clean sheets on my bed. It made me sad, a little, because I knew they were lies. But I visited, and she came over to my aunt's house, and we hugged and laughed and loved each other greatly and talked for hours on end about everything. Except "stuff." My mom was a terrific metaphysician, extremely interested in the world around her and in the lives of others. She was spiritual even at her darkest moments, and funny even in her greatest sorrows. She was a joy to be around, if you could avoid the stuff.

My mom must've grown tired of moving, because she stayed many years in the little house that she'd moved into while I was away in Tallahassee. I believe her tenure there resulted from a massive conglomeration of coincidences, cosmic synchronicity, and karma. Staying in one home for a number of years was a big bang of sorts, a new beginning that ultimately brought the same end: more stuff.

Mom finally had a place she could easily afford, whether she was working a lot or only a little. Still, she was busy buying "the most amazing things," and bills went unpaid, but her landlord, Joan, would forgive her and frequently let the rent be late for weeks – even months – at a time, until my mom caught up.

Since moving in, Mom had amassed more stuff than she'd had in any one place since we'd moved out of the big house, and just the idea of moving it must have been a difficult, sad, embarrassing task to consider. I wasn't nearby, so she didn't need to keep up appearances for my sake, something she had always seemed to feel a need to do, even though, for my entire upbringing, I had been told that it was unnecessary to maintain appearances among family members, who were supposed to be "real" with each other, honest. So she stayed in Joan's little house, and she lived and worked, and the garage sale sirens kept after her, calling her with their keening songs.

I had a fairly good idea how things were going by what arrived in the mail, or via "Package Express" on a Greyhound bus. My mom never lost the habit of sending care packages – a necessary part of the completely unstructured routine she developed when she lived in Miami and continued when I was away at college. I'd learned over the years that if all of the gifts in the package made sense, she was doing well. If everything in the package still bore the price tags, and she'd included a book she'd already given me scant months before, or a piece of clothing I'd never be caught dead wearing, things were going less well.

I loved her packages, and they usually made me laugh, so I never discouraged the practice, except on the occasions when I knew damned well she couldn't afford to send me anything at all, but even then, my objections bore no weight with her. If I didn't particularly want or need something that arrived in a box, I'd pass it on to a friend who might appreciate it. She'd usually send a card from her current version of The Stack, but the envelope would appear to be too small for the card, bulging at the seams from the clippings, articles, and pages from newspapers, magazines, and local bulletins. She clipped jokes that made her laugh, poems that she thought I'd like, articles about people we'd known and places we'd been together – lighthouses on the East Coast, space shuttle launches, a childhood friend marrying a prominent politician. She also clipped articles about things that she knew my friends liked and sent them along, with little notes like, "This reminded me of Andrea," or "Isn't this the town in Connecticut where Steve is from?" scribbled across the top.

She was also famous for clipping the ends off of Celestial Seasonings tea boxes, because they usually contained some great quotation or sweet saying. She clipped these almost as loyally as she and I had clipped Campbell's soup labels for me to turn in at school, so our class could win free supplies and equipment. I always recognized the Celestial Seasonings clippings as being from these particular boxes of tea because, well, she always sent me tea, too. And it was always Celestial Seasonings, unless the tea included Earl Grey, in which case it was nearly always Twining's.

Please don't misunderstand me, and please don't be afraid to offer me tea, should we ever have the chance to visit together on a cool autumn evening. I love a nice cup of tea, and find something very soothing about preparing the water, steeping the bags in a teapot, and filling the cup, sometimes adding honey or lemon, but only ever real sugar and milk for me with Earl Grey. I like the presentation, the warm vapors rising to my nose from the cup as I slowly and deeply inhale the leaves, the herbs, the bits of flowers that season my water. So it's not strange that my mom sent tea: I liked it, and she knew I did, so why not, right? Right! But she'd send several boxes every time she sent me something, which was more tea than I could drink, more tea than I could serve and still have a life outside of serving tea. At one point, I owned no fewer than two boxes of every variety of Celestial Seasonings tea on the market.

My mom's care packages usually reflected some little corner of her disorganized mind. She'd include a couple of candles, pretty ones, maybe, hand-dipped or made with organic soy or something. But she'd send them to me in a box along with some books she'd found at a secondhand bookstore, maybe about theatre or Salvador Dali, or an old, gold-leafed copy of Longfellow poems, which I knew wasn't worth anything, but it was ornate and beautiful, and she'd thought of me. And some hard candies. All sent lovingly – by bus if she felt manic, or third-class postage if not. From Florida. In the middle of summer.

So I'd open a box with great anticipation, made greater by the lovely lavender or patchouli or lemon scent from the candles inside, only to find the hard candies less than hard, and the candles melted over the pages of the books, an inseparable ball of wisdom and wax. I'd laugh at my disappointment, and then I'd cry just a little because I knew she hadn't considered this possible outcome, and because I knew that I'd have to break the news to her.

From time to time, she'd mail things to my friends, too. The ones to whom she sent things usually thought it was very sweet and thoughtful, and they rarely understood the caution with which the words "What did she send, exactly?" came out of my mouth.

Only two friends ever got things that were worth any negative mention: Andrea got an envelope of clippings – good ones – but the whole thing reeked of cat piss. She was nice enough to assume, out loud and in my presence, that something had happened in transit – "Some feral cats must've gotten into a mail truck. Poor mailman!" – and laughed it off. Our eyes met at one point, and we both knew what we were afraid to say, but it was far too unfamiliar and frightening to address. Not yet, and not aloud, anyway.

The other problematic gift from my mom went to a Kelly and Lee, couple who were my friends and neighbors. I'd gone to school with Kelly, and we were close, so we kept a loving and watchful eye out for each other's homes and welfare. It was Christmas 1995, and I was working and busily rehearsing a theatrical production. Getting away to "home" in Florida seemed like an imposition on my oh-so-productive life, so I'd invited my mom to fly up for the holidays – my treat. I thought it would be fun, different, and certainly less depressing than going back to my hometown, certain that I wouldn't be invited into my mom's house full of stuff if she could avoid it. I invited her to Atlanta for the holidays because despite all of Mom's stuff, her lifelong insistence that she wasn't "very smart," and her moods – which now shifted more swiftly than a tornado's direction, thanks to chemical *and* hormonal imbalances – she was still one of my favorite people in the world.

My mom had always been the best hostess she could possibly be, given whatever means she had to host with. She was overly generous, spared no manageable expense, and would give up her own bed, couch, and floor for guests, even if it meant sleeping in her car for the night. She was equally as good a guest, and would never arrive to anyone's home for a meal – be it a friend, relative, or stranger – without bringing along a gift, or more than one. Flowers bought or picked stealthily from a neighboring yard were always a good bet, or a bottle of wine – unless the host was a known alcoholic – or maybe some dessert or fresh fruit or a tape of some piece of music she liked and wanted to share. She never arrived empty-handed, and the Christmas I invited her to Atlanta was no different.

Getting her to town was already a problem when I picked her up at Hartsfield Airport that day. She'd been supposed to arrive two days prior. It had taken me a full 24 hours to realize that the delay she said she'd suffered had been a ruse.

It shouldn't have taken so long. I had experience with these things and should have known the signs. She'd missed enough school concerts, plays, graduations, and award ceremonies. That's not to say that she hadn't attended plenty; she had. But sometimes the world would get the better of her, and her strong, fighter's spirit would be dragged down deep, drowning in the smallness of the situation. Held near the bottom, unable to gasp for air in the liquid uncertainty of those passing moments, she never knew how to signal for help. She seemed to think lifeguards were the enemy, so she'd flounder, alone, hoping to be thrown ashore by the oncoming·tide. I recognized it as depression, and knew that somewhere inside herself she was, in fact, fighting – for herself, for me. But, as often as not, I also called it "selfishness," because her depression seemed to get the best of her when I needed her most.

This visit was no different. I'd made plans for us, had lined up fun things to do, and had arranged to spend Christmas Day at Kelly and Lee's, along with some other friends and family, playing games, laughing, and really enjoying the day. I felt – perhaps finally – grown up. I was managing my life, if not always easily, and coming into my own. I'd developed relationships, held down a job, had friends and artistic connections, and was as close to paying off both my student loans and the IRS as I'd ever been. I wanted Mom to celebrate Christmas with me, while I celebrated that I was learning to live my life.

I'd called her five times the night before her flight was scheduled: no answer. I'd called the morning of her flight: no answer. I sat in my apartment, staring at the phone and out the window, wondering whether to go to the airport. I called again. Stared some more. Finally, 30 minutes after her flight was supposed to take off, my phone rang. Her "Hi" told me everything I needed to know. She tried to tell me a story about her washing machine at the laundromat breaking and not spinning properly and having to move the clothes and rewash all of her laundry and, as a result, missing her flight. It was a long story with lots of phony details, but she knew by my lack of surprise and flat response – "So, are you coming at all?" – that I wasn't buying it and was upset.

Two days later, Mom finally managed to get on a flight and showed up with no suitcase: just two large tote bags, one with a zipper and one with things piled up and spilling out of the top. Somehow, security had let one bag pass as her purse. She had layered herself in two blouses, a turtleneck, and a sweater because Atlanta was having a little cold snap. She wore a skirt, though, like she almost always did, and socks pulled halfway up her calves, underneath her Birkenstock shoes. She looked like she was either wealthy, chic, and eccentric or a bag lady. I waved at her when I saw her, mumbling under my breath, "Really?"

Thinking twice as much about others as about herself, Mom had managed, as usual, to bring something for everyone who'd be at the party the next day – Kelly and Lee, as well as Kelly's folks, our friend Andrea and her roommate Jane – and even Andrea's dad. In the bottom of the zipped tote was a second skirt, some underwear and socks, two more sweaters and a turtleneck – she'd sleep in her slip – her wallet, and a hairbrush with several rubber bands wrapped around the handle. Everything else she'd carried was for someone else. She asked me, as she got in the car, if I had any giftwrap, or if we might stop and pick some up. Did I mention that her flight had landed at 11:52 p.m. on Christmas Eve?

The next day, we arrived, with wine and gifts in tow, at Kelly and Lee's door. A lovely day was had by all, though sometime after dinner, my mom reported that she felt ill and needed to retire to my home next door. I gave her the key and saw her off, thanking her for being there and giving her a warm, deep hug. I stayed behind to drink wine and play games into the wee hours. This is when the embarrassment of my mother's riches came to light.

She'd given everyone a Christmas card earlier that day. Though the envelopes had all been just a little yellowed, and the glue on the flaps less than sticky, the cards were sweet, and each had a handwritten sentiment before my mom's signature: Jonelle. (Though she'd found out that her name was spelled "Jonell" on her original birth certificate, she'd kept the "e" that she'd been taught to spell it with for most of her life, only ever signing "Jonell" during a particularly rebellious period.)

Most of my friends received some sort of handmade ornament from the bounty of the bottomless tote bag – a charm for a necklace, a charm for the tree – hand-painted, crocheted, decoupaged – and each was attached to the corner of their Christmas card with a simple ribbon or strand of red yarn. I'd had some giftwrap, but I'm still uncertain where the ribbons and yarn came from. That was my mother – creating something from nothing.

The hosts were the reason Mom had needed the giftwrap; she'd brought something for the Kelly and Lee, the couple generous enough to open their home to us on the holiday, and she felt it deserved wrapping. It was a special type of chocolate, shaped like an orange, which presents itself as a whole fruit, but with one rap on a table, it splits into sections that each look like a real orange section robed in chocolate. Mom had always found this candy unique, and although she would rarely buy one for herself, it was a gift she loved to give. Something about it symbolized kinship and union to her, the parts of the whole.

My mom had been gone for awhile, and dessert had faded from memory when one of the hosts remembered the chocolate, and opened it.

There's a thing that happens to chocolate. I've never asked a chocolatier why, but I remember seeing something about it on The Cooking Channel or Food Network. Chocolate turns kind of white, or chalky, I think when it gets too old, or is heated up and cooled again (and again and again, maybe). Or maybe it happens when the chocolate gets buried and forgotten underneath a foot of clothing trampled by 7 cats and stacked on top of a milk crate full of matchbox cars in poor condition and 2 Stretch Armstrong dolls sitting just next to 9 cast iron skillets and a bag of 32 packs of cocktail napkins with "Class of '89" printed on them (even though she knew no one who had graduated in 1989), all resting beside the 5 Styx albums she'd bought at least 10 times, because she remembered that I loved them but forgot that I owned all of those albums in every form in which they had ever been available, including a now-broken cassette tape that I still intend to splice.

Whatever it is, at any rate, that happens to chocolate had happened to this Christmas gift chocolate. Lee had opened the discolored chocolate in the kitchen, but he wasn't gone long. Returning to the living room, where we all scribbled clues for the next round of our party game, he offered, "More wine? Anybody? Neal, how's your beer holding out?" No one else had heard him mention the chocolate or knew he'd gone to open it. No one else had noticed that he had come back empty-handed. I was always hyper-aware of what could go wrong when Mom wasn't "right."

When I thought an appropriate interval had passed, I excused myself to the restroom and made a pass through their kitchen "to get a glass of ice water" on my way back to the game. On the corner of the counter, resting on top of my giftwrap, was the chocolate in its foil wrapper. I peeked inside and noticed that its grandeur had been reduced to a chalky white orb as unappetizing as rotten citrus. I picked up the box and foil and turned toward the garbage can, ready to do away with the mess she'd made, when I noticed something else: In addition to the chocolate's appearance, the exterior of the box had a very slight odor, a soupçon of scent, barely noticeable. Once noticed, however, it was unmistakable: cat piss, the same odor I'd caught a whiff of at the airport. The same liquid that had stained the unremoved price tag on the bottom of the pretty tin box she'd brought me.

My mother, the woman who in my childhood had insisted that my baby-fine hair be brushed, combed, and tended to several times a day so it wouldn't appear unruly, was living in cat piss.

Merry Christmas.

I was angry, and as frightened by this gift as I'd been by cascades of books and buttons more than a decade before. I threw the entire gift in the trash, said a quick prayer that Lee had only seen it and not *smelled* it, and returned to the game.

Later that night, Mom and I had a terrible fight because she wanted to go home to St. Pete and insisted on leaving right away. (The bluest of the holiday blues had a firm hold on her. In retrospect,

I understand that she didn't want to "fake it," and she especially didn't want me to see her pain and sorrow.)

I refused to take her to the airport to await a flight on standby. She cried. She called a taxi. I lost my cool. She cried. I told her that if she was going to come and visit again in the future, she should leave her cat piss-soaked presents behind.

The taxi came. She left. I cried.

We didn't talk for two weeks, a desert of time.

The day after Christmas, I apologized profusely for Mom's "gift" to our hosts; they were gracious and understanding, though all of us were only just beginning to understand.

CHAPTER 9

Coping

By the spring of 1997, I'd met my first husband, Adam, who lived outside of Chicago, and we were carrying on a long-distance courtship. We'd already had many discussions about how we could end up in the same city someday, and which city that would be. He hadn't met my family yet – not one of them. I hadn't told him too terribly much about them. I was busy enjoying being in love. I didn't want him to think I'd caught their kind of crazy; my own was bad enough. He had no idea what I'd be facing when I finally got the call from my family telling me that my mother was definitely not okay.

Linda was the one who called to tell me that Mom was no longer letting anyone into her home. Of course she was. Linda was strong. She would do what she knew had to be done when the rest of the family was crumbling around her. Linda was the only one with enough fortitude to take our mortally ill family pets to the vet "when the time came," and there were many pets, and many "times."

My brother Casey and Aunt Linda had been trying to reach Mom for weeks, and she'd stopped returning calls. They knew that she was alive, and that she was coming and going from her home. Sometimes her car was there, sometimes not. They knew she was doing some in-home healthcare work, and they saw her car at her workplace, but she never returned calls.

Mom finally answered the door one evening after Linda knocked and knocked, and called out, over and over. But she wouldn't let Linda in the house.

Linda was worried. Mom had already developed diabetes and was terrible about self-care. She rarely took her blood sugar, and when she did, the numbers often rang in at 300, 400, and up. She was first diagnosed because she "wasn't feeling well," had "a terrible headache," and felt "weak" – so weak she thought she'd best not drive herself to the hospital so instead of calling 911, she took a taxi. Her arrival at the ER prompted them to take her blood sugar immediately. It was 1200. She should have been dead, but my mom was nothing if not strong. ("Strong," to me, seemed to be one of the greatest things one could be. When I was in college, one of my many goodie boxes contained a clipping - an ad extracted from a magazine. It was a photograph of an enormous lion, striding through water, and beneath it were printed the words "This is how strong you are." In the corner she'd written, "I love you, Mom." I keep that picture, still, as a reminder of her confidence in me, although the ballpoint ink fades more and more each year.)

Mom's bipolar disorder, now diagnosed but basically untreated, was always cause for concern as well. She wouldn't make all of her doctor appointments, often because she felt like they weren't listening to her. Medicaid coverage was all that she had, so her options for care were few. Most of the medications came with side effects that she did not adjust to well, so eventually she would stop taking them.

We knew, and we watched, and we worried. When her darkness would fall, we often feared we'd not find her again in that starless night in her mind. But she'd always come back.

I'd talked to my mom numerous times in the weeks before Linda told me about not being allowed in the house. Mom never mentioned that anything was wrong. She evaded some direct questions, half-answered others, but seemed generally alright. I didn't want to alarm her, or let on that I'd been told about the probable state of her home, so I decided to play along – like everything was fine – and planned a visit.

I'd been picked up at the airport before in her vehicles, which were usually loaded to the brim with stuff. On one occasion, when for some reason I'd flown home from college instead of driving, I clearly recall the discomfort of riding atop my suitcase all the way home from the Clearwater airport. This was, frankly, because the only excess room in the car, aside from the space occupied by my mother driving the heap of moving violations, was the two-thirds of the passenger seat occupied by my suitcase and me. I was plenty for a passenger seat to handle at nearly all times in those years, and my sitting atop a suitcase meant somehow staring, neck wrenched sideways, at the torn headliner of the AMC station wagon most of the way home.

Mom drove a low-rider. She hadn't altered her vehicle: She'd simply overwhelmed it with stuff. You name it: newspapers, shoes, laundry gone so stale that it ceased to be classifiable as laundry. Then, during a manic spell, she had decided to do some volunteer work, so she started working with a local organization called "Second Table" or something like that, that helped congregate dining rooms. The charity did great work, retrieving items nearing expiration from local bakeries and grocery stores and delivering them to local halfway houses and soup kitchens, so food didn't go to waste. Excellent charity, excellent idea – an excellent way for my mom to spend time, make a difference, and feel useful.

Except.

Somehow, as it always did with her, the idea transformed. Grew. Took on new life and added potential. She had the revelation one day that she passed the needy, the homeless, and the hungry on the streets nearly every day in St. Petersburg. There was always the potential, at any interstate exit, to encounter a soul in a very unfortunate position. So she would help. She would – as she always wanted to – save them. She would become her own entity, an unauthorized, very nonprofit and unprofitable charity on wheels: a traveling soup kitchen.

So she held back some items here and there. Scratch-and-dent cans would go to the homeless shelter – except for a few. Bread and pastries donated generously by the bakery manager at the local Publix would be dropped at the soup kitchen – save a handful of boxes, and so on.

Except.

It was a really great idea until the bread went stale, the pastries grew mold, and then the boxes grew together and ended up under cans of food, under newspapers, under other boxes of other moldy pastries. Mom always intended to give it all away. But she would get tired, or be running late for work, and she'd forget that the pastries were there. She'd remember later, usually the next day. Unfortunately, then, on her way to give them away, or feed them to the ducks, she'd find a yard sale, and suddenly, a wicker plant stand she *had* to buy was being shoved in on top of the baked goods. So they'd be forgotten again, for days – or weeks, if she happened to get depressed in the meantime.

You get the idea: a health department violation on wheels.

I can only be grateful that during my years living in her home, the stuff in the car was never food-like and, therefore, although abundant, it was never moldy.

So this is what I'd expected to pick me up when I came to town for my visit from Atlanta. (I nearly wrote, "This was what I'd grown accustomed to and expected to pick me up" but had to stop and correct myself. I never really grew accustomed to it. It always made me uncomfortable. But she was so strong and so fragile all at once, and I was always afraid to strike a chord that might shatter her. I'd bring up the issue but not push it. I'd suggest cleaning out the car but not demand it. I'd rearranged things and cleaned up a little on past visits but hadn't bitched about the piles of debris that mounted higher and higher, as the miles between us grew greater.)

This time, when I got to the Tampa airport and made my way out to the baggage area, there was no Mom. Instead, I saw my brother Casey. Turned out that Mom's vehicle had reached "inoperable" that week – or so he'd been told – so she'd asked him to do the fetching at the airport. (I discover two days later that the mechanical failure was a ruse because she'd been so depressed for weeks that there was no longer even one-third of a passenger seat in her car. There was a driver's seat, and there was stuff.)

I didn't stay at my brother's house, or at Linda's, even. I went to my mom's house, prepared to face whatever was necessary head-on. I had somehow imagined that with a couple of days of hard work, sweat, and elbow grease, I could emerge some sort of superhero, or at least bald and with a big gold earring like Mr. Clean.

Mom was outside when we arrived, watering her plants. This was a wonder about my mom: Her green thumb could transform the most desolate, barren, hard earth into botanical bliss, her own Garden of Eden. Whatever insanity was taking place, pile by pile, inside of her home, her yard was always a place where things grew, were nurtured, and flourished. Not just green, but *lush*. Foliage more than full: abundant. Flowers more brilliantly colored than any of her neighbors produced, no matter how much they'd paid for them or how pricey their fertilizer. "Volunteer" vegetables sprouted here and there: summer squash next to the zebra plant, and a watermelon vine thriving just beneath some wisteria. It was an unexpected wonder, my mother's yard, and long had been. It was where she seemed to find solace. She could water her plants and be alone, feel quiet inside. In the garden, she could think, or, perhaps more accurately, *not* think, but indulge in the all-too-rare absence of thought. It was as though she'd surrendered her Catholic altar to the wilderness, and now worshiped every leaf, every bough as part of the Greater Thing that she always somehow remembered we were a part of.

So there she was, watering, standing in a blouse limp from humidity, and culottes smeared with soil and a tiny bit of blood from a snagged cuticle. She looked the way she had always looked to me: real. My mother – without pretense, affectation, or propriety. She was as real as anyone I'd ever known, and her dark eyes nearly vibrated with life, even at her worst.

She stopped watering, put down the hose, and came over to hug my brother and me. She thanked him for picking me up, and again addressed the lame excuse she'd concocted about a car problem. He stayed for a few minutes and talked, but made a fairly quick exit. How could he not? She wouldn't let him into the house. She hadn't for months. Why should he stay?

When we went inside, she pushed open the door and went in first, saying, "Careful."

The door only opened about one-third of the way.

"Sorry. Hector" (one of her cats) "climbed up here earlier and knocked this stack of things over. I just haven't gotten down on the floor yet to pick it all up."

Lie.

I pushed my suitcase in before me, thankful that it was no heavier than it was, and simultaneously wondered where I was going to put it. There was stuff everywhere.

The front door of the tiny house opened into a sunroom of sorts, an enclosed porch that had been used by residents as everything from a reading room to an office to a spare bedroom for a friend in need. The room was no more than six-feet deep and eight-feet wide, composed of windows on three sides, from the chair rail to the ceiling. The windows were covered, so from the outside it was hard to tell that the room was full of stuff: stuff leaning on the walls, piles pressing against the windows. Boxes, baskets, handbags and shopping bags full. Magazines. Books. More magazines. Pottery. A macramé owl. Three bent spring-tension curtain rods.

That's what I saw in the first three seconds, all of it together in one place, and my mind started singing the song, "One of These Things is Not Like the Others" from back in my Sesame Street youth. I'm sort of twisted that way. A skill developed, to be sure, as a coping mechanism. I can find nearly anything funny, even when I ought not. Even when finding humor in something could result in public humiliation or, as I have been reminded, death. Death, you ask? Indeed. Allow me to explain:

I graduated from Florida State University at the end of the spring semester, 1991. I'd pursued the worthwhile, though not particularly gainful, art of theatre. The FSU graduating class was so large that commencement ceremonies were held at the Civic Center. As we filed into the hall and found our seats, the 20 or so of us graduating from the School of Theatre were dwarfed by the School of Business, which consumed every seat in the upper rear portion of the auditorium. The guest speaker for our ceremony was to be none other than the media magnate of the moment, Ted Turner.

I take ceremony seriously. I try not to laugh at funerals, cough when altar boys pass with incense, or distract any member of a holy procession. I was embarrassed to tears in childhood when, as the flower girl for my aunt Becky's wedding, I was overcome during the practice ceremony with a volcanic fit of flatulence, farting with every step as I walked down the aisle. Every step, that is, until my soon-to-be uncle Gary was roaring with laughter, and even the priest was beginning to crack. I could not stop. They kept coming, unforgiving, as though I was consuming, digesting, and releasing gas from an entire field of raw cabbage with every movement. As the laughter of the wedding party grew, I fell from embarrassed to mortified and ran, crying, back up the aisle and out of the church.

So it's not like me to want to disrupt an otherwise auspicious occasion, but there was something about the day of my college graduation. As we found our seats, I was light inside, happy, feeling buoyant and fully forgetful of the impending period of almost certain unemployment that lay before me. I was seated beside a close friend, Kava, who shared my often-inappropriate sense of humor. We sat, listening dutifully and seriously, to the speakers, the dean of students, and other esteemed guests. Finally, the time came for Ted Turner to speak.

Never, in the history of commencements, has anyone delivered a less applicable speech. Riding on the right-wing economic policy coattails of the Wall Street and BMW 1980s, Turner delivered a speech to us about how to go forth and prosper. And prosper some more. The crux of it, as I remember, went something like this: "Graduates, now you're done with school. Go out and get a job and make some money. Once you have that money, make some more money. Because with that money, you can then make even more money. Money. Money. Money. And, lest you forget, make money."

Perhaps it was not despite, but rather because of, the speaker's infamy that I got the giggles. Here he was, a multi-millionaire addressing thousands upon thousands of people, and nearly every other word out of his mouth was "uh." So the speech sounded more like, "Uh, good, uh, afternoon, uh, graduates. Today marks, uh, an auspicious and uh . . ." and so on. The pauses and "uhs" were so frequent, so predictable, that it was difficult not to mock him. Impossible, really. So we began: With every "uh" of Ted's, Kava and I simultaneously voiced our own quiet "uh." The first few were amusing, making us crack a smile. As it went on, though, our smiles were all but erupting into bouts of giggles. A few of our classmates, the ones nearest us, could hear. A few of them began to chuckle, too, ever so quietly.

And then, reality: One of our other classmates, Barbara, seated almost directly in front of us, turned, smiling, and whispered: "Careful, ladies. That man has so much money, he could have you killed."

It was a joke. It was funny. But it was very, very true. A return to solemnity settled upon us.

So, years later, as I was entering my mom's house with Sesame Street's "One of These Things is Not Like the Other" running through my head, it didn't strike me as unusual. I recognized my coping mechanism and thanked God for it. By the looks of things there, it was going to be much needed.

CHAPTER 10

Noah

Past the "sunroom," where I'd stashed my suitcase – blocking the front door and praying there wouldn't be a fire – was the living room. Full. There was a path through the room, about three feet wide. Mom, it was clear, had been working that day to make space for me.

At the time, her couch was an old rattan thing with three seat cushions, and there was a matching chair as well. I could tell that was where she sat. The chair was cleared off, near the table that held her telephone and a lamp. It was across the path from the shelf where her television sat, and on the table beside her chair were a couple of telltale signs of her roosting: newspaper clippings, her address book, and several pens next to a spiral notebook. She'd cleared room for me, too. One and one-half cushions of the couch were clear, save the two cats lounging on them. The other half of the couch was full of clothes, towels, sheets – clean laundry, she told me, that she'd just taken to the laundromat that day.

The other end of the room was once her dining area. The dining room table and chairs were still there, and her sewing machine was still sitting on the table, ready to use, but buried beneath months of acquisitions:

She'd bought boxes of mason jars and what looked like a dozen skeins of yarn, and had excuses for all of them. "I thought I'd do some canning this year, and maybe get back into crochet," she said.

When I eyed a stack of model airplane kits, resting on top of a bunch of Shrinky Dink boxes, she said, "I was thinking maybe the Police Athletic Club could use the models? Maybe we'll take them down while you're home? And the Shrinky Dinks – well, Sarah's too old. Maybe Matt or Kevin would have fun with them? Oh, and there's this. . ." She pulled a calligraphy kit from amidst the other things. "Do you still like to do calligraphy?"

I shrugged. I thought that there must have been a hobby store going out of business somewhere in St. Pete.

The bookshelf and desk that had been across from the table still appeared to be present, though I couldn't be sure because of the mountains that lay around it.

"I've got a bunch of Ann Tyler books there," she said. "I think I have them all now. I've read them if you want to take them home."

It was a funny thing about the stuff: She was so attached to it, yet constantly trying to give it away. She was obsessed with obtaining, but nearly as eager to find a home for all of the things she obtained:

Baby dolls without little girls – or boys, for that matter – to play with them. A rural library's volume of books, but not enough eyes to read them. Bolts of fabric to make enough Dress Up Day clothes for every child in the local elementary school.

Piles of good intentions, mountains of them. More than she could give away.

The kitchen was accessible past the dining area, and used to open on to a back porch. I say used to, because a couple of the piles on the porch had slid, collided, and collapsed in front of the door. Now, if you wanted to get to the back porch, you had to go outside, but there wasn't a whole lot of point in doing that, as there was really no porch, only stuff. The back porch was enclosed, like the sunroom. Some of the windows leaked ever so slightly, but no one could get *to* them in order to repair them, so they continued to leak. She didn't report it to the landlady, of course, because that would mean someone would have to come in and see her stuff. So, water from the small leaks seeped inside, and now the porch smelled something like rotten paper and a roofer's undeodorized armpits.

The kitchen was full, too, but it didn't strike me as disgusting. There was very, very little space.

Clean dishes, pots, pans, small appliances – five juicers, three blenders, two toaster ovens, and six stick blenders – were piled everywhere. But half of the split sink was empty, and there was dish soap. She'd washed the dishes she'd used, and they were drying on the dish rack in the other half of the sink. Okay, so she was bananas, I thought, but at least she wasn't gross. (I hadn't seen the moldy car pastries yet, nor the bathroom, and whatever I *would* see on this trip wasn't going to be anything compared with what was to come. Eventually, my mother *was* gross, even to me, sometimes. So are disgusting baby diapers, yet parents have dealt with them since time immemorial. Gross is nothing. Gross is like ugly is like pretty is like stinky. Gross is only an adjective. My mom was a noun.)

Having toured half of the house in my first 90 seconds inside, I excused myself to the tiny bathroom, which was directly off the living room on a short hallway that connected the two bedrooms. When I opened the bathroom door, I smelled the telltale sign of Mom's cleaning: Pine Sol. Okay, so she'd just cleaned the bathroom. As I sat on the toilet to pee, I tried not to hit my head on the shelf that hung above it – or on the shelf that hung next to it – or on the one in front of it. It seemed every possible inch of wall space had been filled with bric-a-brac shelving, which in turn had been filled – every possible inch – with stuff:

Vick's VapoRub, times five. Tiny cobalt blue glass jars filled with marbles. Colored glass jars in the windowsill full of peacock feathers from Aunt Catty's farm and sea oats. (She's not in possession of them now so I'll tell you: Mom picked sea oats. Twice. Wild rebel, she was.) Rolls of gauze and tape, several pair of safety scissors, and, of course, a stethoscope. Dishes with guest soaps, several of them, in that tiny bathroom.

Bananas.

I remember that the only positive thought I could muster was, "Well, at least the shower works."

The rest of the house was in similar condition – stuffed to the gills with things, all useful but too plentiful. The front bedroom, where I was to sleep, had a single bed, which had been cleared for me. There was a dresser, but it was full, Mom said, of spools of thread and things my brother, Carl, had left behind on his last brief stay in her home. I couldn't understand why she'd kept them, especially since there were things of mine that she was *supposed* to have kept and didn't. Things I treasured: a childhood doll collection with some lovely and – as the apple doesn't fall far from the tree – some very unusual and eclectic dolls. Not baby dolls, but Campbell's soup dolls, cornhusk dolls, and hand-sewn sock dolls with sweetly smiling embroidered faces – dolls that came with stories, or suggested them, even dolls that came with little books – all gone, lost in some move or damaged in some garage, carport, storage space, closet, box. Not that it mattered, except that it did.

So my stuff, what little I'd wanted to keep, was gone, but there was Carl's, filling a dresser. My brother had, as far as I knew, not contacted Mom for years unless he needed something – usually money or shelter, or both – but I suppose she felt she owed him. Mom was always doing that – compensating now for things she'd done in the past, for mistakes that she'd made. She'd sold Carl's coin collection, but denied it, years before. Because she'd pawned off what he valued then, she'd make up for that now by holding on to his stuff.

It didn't make sense, really, and it wasn't like the score was, or could be, or even *needed* to be, settled. But she'd still try to, always – doing penance for her sins, seeking forgiveness and absolution.

I didn't even know if it was really his stuff in the dresser, anyway. She might have lied. I couldn't tell and wouldn't have looked, even if I could get to the dresser.

But I couldn't.

Or to the bookshelf.

I could barely reach the lamp on the bedside table so that I could read myself to sleep that night. I was also afraid of turning it on. I wasn't sure what wattage the bulb was and was a little concerned about setting something on fire. There were, among other things, a bunch of scarves in a basket on the table near the lamp. At age 12, while babysitting a toddler, I had laid a scarf over a lamp, trying to soften the light and get the child to sleep. The damn thing caught on fire or, really, melted. I put the fire out, and the house didn't burn down, but I was never called to babysit there again. I never even told the mom when she got home and drove me to my house. I guess she missed her scarf, or smelled the melted polyester. I liked that lady, so it was a bummer.

I've never told anyone that before.

Anyway, there I was, later that night in my mom's house, reading who-knows-what that I'd plucked off a shelf to get myself to sleep, and there she was, in her room at the other end of the hall, snoring.

The path through the hall was crowded, which would seem impossible, as the hall was about 5-feet long and 3½-feet wide, and had to accommodate four doorways: to the living room, bathroom, and both bedrooms. There are not a lot of ways to fill the space that's not taken by doorframes, right? She'd fit in two corner shelves and hung baskets off every available wall space. The baskets were, of course, full of things:

Spare toothbrushes, tiny bottles of shampoo that would have come from hotels, except that she never stayed in hotels at that point in her life. She probably got them at a garage sale – a little, unused remnant of someone else's travels. Coupons. A tire gauge. Spanish moss. Air plants. Booklets and fliers.

Dried flowers picked on her last adventure to Sarasota or Lutz or Citrus County. A syringe or two, as she was a fully insulin-dependent diabetic by then and always had syringes around.

In retrospect, I can see that my mom was keeping too much stuff long before we ever had to move T.C.'s stuff out of the garage, before we ever moved and moved and moved. My whole family used to joke about it when I was young, every time Monty Hall would head out into the audience on "Let's Make a Deal" and ask some anxious audience member to produce – oh, who knows? – a boiled egg, a tube of red lipstick, a piece of aluminum foil, an after-dinner mint – from her purse. If the woman in the audience had that object, there was always a generous cash prize and excitement from her friends and family. My brothers and I told Mom she should catch a bus to Hollywood and go to a filming of the show. We were dead certain she'd win a bunch of money for all of the things that could emerge from her bag: a collapsible drinking cup, a bottle of aspirin or Tylenol, a pair of safety scissors, Band-Aids, dental floss, three unmatched buttons, thread and a needle, ChapStick, Tiger balm, a brooch – now broken – several tattered pieces of paper with notes, phone numbers, dates, and times scribbled on them, a hardboiled egg (yes, sometimes). Mom laughed along with us, because she was capable of holding two truths in one space. Her purse *was* too full. At the same time, she believed that on any given day she might actually need one of the sundry things inside to rescue herself, or her family, from disaster. She was an urban survivalist, and her purse was her away-from-home emergency kit. It was the smaller version of her stuff.

I lay in her house that night, listening to her snore through her bedroom door, cracked open not because she chose not to close it, but because she no longer could. The piles had fallen in front of it, too, blocking it open and blocking it closed. She sort of crawled into her room through the crack, scaling sideways against a pile to her bed, of which she maintained a fair quarter clear enough to sleep on.

She snored deeply – she always had – and she slept so soundly, it was if she wasn't even there, save for the loud sawing. Her body was almost hollow, lifeless except for its breathing; she was so very far away in her dreams. She believed in astral projection, and though she rarely consciously attempted to do so, she frequently found herself wandering outside of her body as she slept. (I won't say she didn't. If anyone might, it would be she.) To wake her was, for me, always a little scary. She would, more often than not, wake with a start, eyes flying open as though she'd seen a ghost, or an alien – a gasping, frightened, guttural sound, like the sound I remember coming from Donald Sutherland's mouth at the end of the 1970's remake of "Invasion of The Body Snatchers." If you didn't know her, or didn't know it was coming, it would shock you enough to make you scream right back at her. Next, there was a second where everything, everyone, in the room just stopped – frozen. Then, suddenly, she was awake – wiping her eyes, registering who was before her and that she'd come back to her body again.

The next day, I woke up, lamp still on and book in hand, thinking about coffee and cleaning her kitchen.

"Susan, you don't have to . . ."

"I *do* have to. *And* I want to, Mom. It's why I'm here."

"Well, I just –"

"Just nothing," I said, through the rattling of multiple sheet pans. "Don't worry. I won't get rid of anything priceless, Mom."

"Well, I know. But . . ."

I stopped moving things and turned to look at her. I took her hands in mine. "Mom, I love you. But you can't live like this."

I could see the shame well up in her, and there didn't seem to be any way to avoid it. I wasn't trying to shame her. I wasn't even trying to change her, really, I didn't think. I didn't expect that upon my departure she'd suddenly begin living the life of a monk, with spare possessions and space abundant around her being. I didn't imagine she'd stop going to garage sales altogether, or stop spending money on things that were ridiculously cool yet terribly unnecessary. I didn't imagine that her self-care would improve greatly, or that she'd begin spending her money on things like Depends. (She'd started experiencing bladder leaks and had been resorting to layers of folded-over washcloths that had to be changed frequently and had no odor-masking capability at all. I discovered with sadness and frustration the diaper pail-like corral of her personal hygiene cloths of choice later during that trip, previously masked by that strong scent of Pine Sol when I'd arrived.)

I knew my mom was, fundamentally, who she was, and I loved that. I also knew that, for a lot of her life, she had been able to be who she was and still maintain a home that could be safely navigated, front door to back, without running the risk of personal injury or death by avalanche.

I put my arms around her and hugged her tight, telling her again that I loved her, and I was only there to help. I felt how her body had changed, a little thinner, a little frailer in her embrace. She was aging, and I finally had enough distance to see it. She was only 59, but her hardscrabble years, frequently ignored diabetes, and unchecked mental strain had aged her. She was still vibrant and full of life, but smaller somehow, like a statue that's been broken and mended over and over, losing little pieces every time.

Her carpal tunnel syndrome was more and more evident, her fingers going numb faster than ever before with sustained movement. She never mentioned it, but I saw the way she shook her hands, massaged them, rubbed her fingertips together as if, like a Girl Scout with a flint, she might rub them enough to spark something in them again. I never quite understood why she thought these behaviors would improve the situation until I wrecked my own wrists and started shaking my hands, rubbing them, massaging my fingertips. Then I got it: We're animals licking a wound, trying to do something that instinct says might help. We aren't all studied in the multitude of nerve pathways or myofascial release. Whatever hurts, we just want it to stop hurting, and we shake until it does. We want the feelings back, the ones we once had, and we wring our hands to extract them from the thirsty past.

The kitchen was so full that there was no way we could work on it together, and it would simply have been too painful, watching her watching me, feeling her feeling judged, when I just wanted her to be able to use her oven, her stove, her cabinets. I get it, that that's a form of judgment, too. I get that I was trying to impose my will on her. "But for Chrissakes – really," I thought. "You can't even see what you have. How can you use it, enjoy it? And moreover, I cannot not see you live like this. It's dangerous. It's ludicrous. It's *embarrassing*."

I didn't say any of those things out loud. I thought about almost every word I said for the four days I was there. My presence, my actions, were hurtful enough. I didn't want my words to do further damage. So I worked quietly, listening to the radio that she had playing outside as she worked in the garden. She had amassed a pile of belongings outside of her home now as well. It was hidden from the street, but it was there, so her task for the days of my visit was to work at going through that pile.

"Just get rid of the things that are really bad, okay, Mom? Like the stuff that's broken and can't be repaired. Or the stuff that is wet, like wet cardboard or stuff, you know, that's literally falling apart."

The kitchen was, in a way, miraculous. I felt like I'd wandered into the tale of the fish and the loaves, except this tale was of the cookie sheets and the loaf pans. Like Tribbles, they seemed to be multiplying faster than I could remove them from the home. I stacked them and stacked them, and then I found more. And when the stacks were high, and I thought my task was complete, I opened a door, a cabinet, a drawer, looked behind a microwave cart or above a refrigerator, and voila! MORE! My mother, it seemed, was prepared to bake for the entire city at once. I counted 34 full-size cookie sheets before I'd found the whole collection.

All in all there were 17 loaf pans, but 4 of them were Pyrex, 1 was cast iron, and there were three "really good nonstick ones." She'd come in to use the bathroom and caught me marveling at the variety. She reminded me about the difference between them, like they were spools of thread or citrus trees.

"Don't go just tossing them out willy-nilly. Please, Sue? I have to have a Pyrex as well as a metal. They cook differently . . . "

"I know," I said.

"And the nonstick are no good for some things, but they're good for quick breads. Unless it's cornbread, in which case, the cast iron. Or the Pyrex. But I do like the nonstick for making monkey bread . . . You know, you'd better keep at least two of each."

"Why two, Mom?"

"Monkey bread."

I rolled my eyes. I could not, in all of my memories of countless bountiful meals, remember my mother making monkey bread.

"And parties, you know? Holidays. And gifts. I love to give away banana bread. You know, it's just as easy –"

"To make two loaves as one," I said. If you can't overdo something, why bother doing it at all? "Yes, Noah," I nodded. "Two of everything on the ark." But two was better than eleven, so I forged on.

"Mom?" I asked, a minute later. "There's only one cast iron one. Should we go get another? How will it breed?"

She gave me a look that said "smarty pants" before she laughed and walked back outside, into her garden. I laughed, hard, for my sanity, and turned back to my work.

It appeared, looking at the plates and bowls stacked all over the stove and counters – among the pots and pans and canned goods, storm candles, thermoses and shopping bags – that she had four different sets of dishes. I don't mean that she had some mismatched shabby-chic thing going on. I mean she appeared to have four entire sets of dishes. It looked like she still had the set I'd bought for her back when I was working retail during college. It was a very popular pattern in the '80s, kind of a farm pattern with barns and animals and tractors scattered around the rims of the plates. I'd chosen it for her because it reminded me of her mother's dishes, which had been yellow, with farm designs "drawn" on in black. She'd had one of her mother's plates displayed on the wall, plaque-like, as long as I could remember, and I remembered her telling me that she and her brothers and sisters had saved up their money to buy the yellow plates for her mother, so I'd thought it was only fitting that I continue the tradition.

But now, added to that set of dishes was a set of "unbreakable" Corelle that we'd used a lot in my youth; when there are 10 to 12 plates on the dinner table, and most of them are for children, a lot of dishes get dropped. There were also some pretty white china plates, scattered with red cherries, and what looked like another full set that were dark brown, tan, and blue; they were heavy and glazed to look like they'd been handmade, but I knew they weren't.

She had 6 cast-iron molds for making individual cornbread loaves shaped like ears of corn. Her kitchen, aside from appliances and cabinetry, was 4-feet wide and 8-feet long, and she had 4 juicers. Huh? ("Someone might need one someday –" I know, I know.)

There were 8 Dutch ovens, 6 4-quart saucepans, 3 teakettles, a total of 46 baking pans (from 8x8 squares to enormous turkey roasting pans, all in at least 2 types of material – usually a metal and a glass.) She'd amassed 5 drawers stuffed full of utensils, from tongs and salad tossing sets to corncob holders and orange juice squeedos – those hard plastic things you stick into the orange so you can suck the juice out. (I call them squeedos thanks to a friend whose brother, in their youth, called him "Squeedo Nose." It's one of those things I've never managed to forget, though I haven't seen that friend in decades.)

Chopsticks, you say? 78 pairs, all stored in mayonnaise jars with no lids.

When I finally felt I'd cleared out the piles in the kitchen to the extent that I could move around in the room, I'd carried nearly two dozen extra-heavy weight lawn and leaf bags full of stuff out of her kitchen. Each bag was as full as I could get it and still be able to lift it by myself. I put the bags in the alley, near the trashcans. I put signs on them, hoping people might take at least some of the items, and praying that the garbage men would come before I'd left town. Otherwise, I knew damn well that my chances were 70/30 that she'd drag all of that shit back inside.

Taking on the food cabinets was next. My stomach churned. It was already beginning to get dark outside, but I didn't really want to stop working. I knew I had a flight to catch in three more days, and the task still ahead seemed insurmountable. Besides, stopping working would mean sitting down, and sitting down would mean looking at the piles of stuff. I really hadn't come to sit, so I started on the cabinets that evening.

I was lucky not to have been crushed to death by the contents of the first one I opened.

I've never hung kitchen cabinets, but I have paid to have a kitchen remodeled. I've seen the bare studs, the drywall placed over them, then the cabinets attached. I've marveled at the physics of wood, at the studs, at how such a small piece of lumber, a tiny slice of a tree, could support so much weight.

But never have I marveled like I marveled that day.

It was as though the entire canned goods section of the scratch-and-dent store had followed her home.

The cabinets in her kitchen were inexpensive ones, the kind of prefabricated sawdust-and-glue stuff that anyone can buy at Home Depot and slap on the wall the same day. They'd been hung a bit too high, so reaching the top shelf was a feat and required a step stool for any but the tallest folk. When I opened the door, something shifted inside and sent a shower of food-filled aluminum catapulting toward my head. I dodged out of the way, and was hit by only one of them – a can of French-cut green beans – though it did double-duty as it ricocheted from my shoulder to the countertop and then down onto the top of my foot. I cursed and picked it up, along with the other cans that had fallen, and began sorting through the makings for stone soup.

The quantity of canned goods was staggering. And, much like cranberry sauce with whole berries, a great number of the items were things I'd never seen my mom eat and doubted that she ever would. There was more condensed and evaporated milk than you can imagine. Did she just forget, on 17 sequential trips to the grocery store, that she already had some? Or was she conspiring to create the largest Tres Leches cake ever baked in the state of Florida?

Was she planning to go on a corn-only diet, or was there another explanation for the 9 cans of creamed corn, 7 cans of sweet kernels, and 1 can of white shoe-peg corn?

Had she been particularly hungry for fish when she purchased the 12 cans of kippers, 8 cans of salmon, and 16 cans of sardines? It appeared from the looks of the cans they'd been there a while. Did she lose interest in canned fish?

The canned goods were easy enough, though. It was really a matter of sorting them into piles, determining whether she could or would really eat them in any reasonable length of time, and hauling many, many bags out of the house, unloading them on the nearest homeless shelter.

It was the dry goods that got me. The cabinet on the other side of the sink was full of them. This was the cabinet in which you might expect dishes to be stored. After all, with only two large cabinets in the kitchen, plus a little cubbyhole above the refrigerator, you'd expect food to occupy one, and the stuff on which to serve food to occupy the other. But Mom was a mistress of the absurd. It appeared that all of her dishes were now stored on the stove, countertops, or the dish drain beside the sink, because the second cabinet was full of dry goods.

I didn't know boll weevils would settle in elbow macaroni. I'd seen them before, a few times, when they'd invaded a sack of flour that wasn't closed properly, and once in a container of cornmeal when the top had accidentally been left ajar. But I didn't know they would like macaroni.

I threw away enough food to feed a small village: sacks of flour – whole-wheat flour, pastry flour, self-rising flour, unbleached flour, potato flour, brown rice flour – boxes and boxes of rice, Rice-A-Roni, macaroni, angel hair pasta, saffron rice, grits, polenta, bulgur wheat, and wheat germ. If it was grain-like and capable of being invaded, it had been, and not only by boll weevils, but also by German cockroaches and, because it was Florida, some palmetto bugs. I tossed all of it into trash bags.

Mom seemed to get more hurt, and at the same time more frenzied, with every bag I carried out. She worked more slowly, but her gaze darted to every bag I carried to the dumpster. She stayed quiet, but questioned me with her eyes. I kept telling her that the things weren't good to eat anymore, that bugs had invaded them, but it didn't seem to matter. She just got sadder. She started watering her plants. By the time I was a teenager she'd taught me, without knowing, that hose water can be great camouflage for tears. Her garden was her favorite place to work and meditate on life. And what are tears but tiny meditations on sadness? That evening, watching her in her yard, I wondered if that's why all of her gardens had always been so lush and green, whether she'd wept them into life.

As evening rolled around, and I'd done away with all of the infested goods, my hunger lurched forward, and my stomach turned. The kitchen was improved, but far from finished, and I couldn't bear the thought of doing more work to make room to prepare a meal, though there was plenty of food in the house! My mother insisted on taking a drive and picking up dinner for us, a grouper sandwich from my favorite local spot, the 4th Street Shrimp Store. I figured it would be good for her to get out of the house for a few minutes, and I also thought it would be a perfect opportunity to call my not-yet-husband back in Chicago.

"Hi, sweetie," Adam answered. "How *are* you?" He had a way of sounding too saccharine, too concerned. I didn't blame him for it, but it irritated me now.

"Tired. And hot, and sweaty. You?"

"Oh," singsong voice, "Everything's good here. Kiki misses you."

He had no idea how little I cared about his cat at that moment. "How's work?" I pressed on, trying to avoid talking about the shitstorm in the center of which I was sitting.

"Oh, fine. Same old same." Long pause, then, "I miss you. I can't wait until you visit again."

I just sighed.

"Is it that bad?" he asked, finally picking up on my mood.

"Yep," I said, and suddenly I felt that tightness in my throat that meant tears were not far behind. "Bad." (I've always found that keeping myself to one-word answers helps to fend off the oncoming tide of holy-crap-here-they-are-anyway tears.) "You have no idea."

He tried to comfort me: "Oh, sweetie, I know."

"NO," I snapped back, "you don't. You don't have any idea. You don't have any idea what it's like, or how sad it is, or how I feel right now, or how goddamned hot this fucking house is, or how hard I've been working all day, or what this place smells like, or anything – " My rage gave way to sobbing.

He was quiet. Smart of him. He waited and waited until I could speak again: "Sorry."

"It's okay," he said.

"Yeah, no, it's not. Sorry. This isn't your fault." Long pause. "I'm gonna go, okay? I love you. I'll be better once I'm done here."

"Okay. I *do* miss you."

"I know," I sighed. "I miss you, too. I miss . . . normal. I miss everything normal."

"Just a few days. Hang in there."

"Yep. Talk to you soon."

I hung up and cleaned my face before Mom came back, hoping the redness would fade so that she wouldn't have something else to be sad about.

Horrible

T he next few days were a blur of sweat and grit and stink, stuff and mold and stuff and broken glass and more stuff. I worked and lifted and packaged and bagged and moved things and rearranged and moved things again. Having grown up an "easier to ask permission than to beg forgiveness" kind of gal, I was operating contrary to all of my training. I tried to sneak out some of the larger items, ones that took up too much square footage, even things I knew that she was the most attached to – just to make some *space*.

I threw away books.

Yes, threw away: not carted to the library, not donated to a school, not taken down to Haslam's Bookstore to be sold in their cherished used book rooms. Expedience was the mission. Triage was all that I could worry about.

I was in some altered state, sandbagging before the storm. I somehow thought – believed even – that if I could make enough space for her to feel what "uncrowded" felt like, surely she'd want to have more space. I believed that I was dropping a stone in a lake, beginning a ripple that would spread and spread until her home was clean and light and full of nothing but space and fresh air. I made enough room to walk all the way around her bed, and there was nothing on the bed but blankets and pillows. No piles. And no piles on the couch. The tiny bathroom was clean, and as orderly as it could be, and the kitchen was functional. Maybe it would be a fresh start. I've always been an optimist.

The last day that I was there, we'd taken showers and cleaned up, dressed and taken a drive out to the beach to watch the sunset. We were sitting on a seawall, watching seagulls dive, ascend, and dive again, when she thanked me.

"I appreciate all of your work the last few days," she said, putting her arm around my shoulders.

"I was happy to help, Mom. I'm always happy to help you."

"I know."

"The truth is, Mom, everyone's always happy to help. People love you. You're an awesome person. You've just got a lot of crap!" I tried to make light of throwing away a third of her stuff.

"I know," she said, not seeming so light herself.

"Really, Mom. I'm not judging you. Okay, maybe I am judging you. I'm trying not to. It's not about you being wrong, Mom. It's just . . . It's not clean. A lot of the stuff I got rid of, it wasn't even –"

"I know."

"I mean, Mom, your kitchen –"

"I know."

It was quiet for a while before she said, "I'm sorry."

Uh-oh. Sorry and sad again. "Please, Mom, don't be sorry. Don't be sad."

"I know."

More quiet, more seagulls, more waves lapping at the sand as the sun slowly sank until she spoke again: "I always think about our house on the beach."

I waited, sure this was leading somewhere.

"I always think about when it burned down." She stared out at the water. "You know, it all kind of happened so fast, but I still remember it all. I remember standing on the sidewalk, watching the flames. Mother was at work, someone had called her, but she hadn't made it home yet. I remember just standing there, on the sidewalk, all of us kids in our pajamas and underwear, watching it burn."

I asked, "Where were the fire trucks?"

"Oh, they weren't there yet."

"So nobody helped?"

She snorted. "Sure. They 'helped.' Before the fire had spread, several people from the neighborhood had come running, making sure all of us kids were out of the house. Then others started running in and out of the house, grabbing what they could, carrying out what they could lift."

"That's good. At least they came."

"Yeah. Except half of everything walked away."

I looked at her. I didn't understand.

"A lot of the stuff that got carried out, we never saw again," she explained. "I remember my mother's mink coat. I don't even know why, but I remember someone coming out of the house with it. I guess because it was one of the nicest things we owned. One of her boyfriends had given it to her, and she almost never wore it – this *is* Florida, after all – but she loved it. She was proud of it. But we never saw it again. That and a bunch of other stuff. Ermine stoles he gave her too, and some jewelry from other boyfriends. Grandmother's silver. Even some furniture. People took it to 'safekeep' it, I guess, but it never came back to us."

I sat silently, listening to the blaze crackling in my mind.

"By the time Mother got home, the whole house was engulfed. The fire crew couldn't save it. How could they? A little wooden house – it burned fast."

The sun had nearly disappeared over the horizon.

"The worst thing was the fish. We had a bowl of goldfish, and someone walked out of the house that night and handed it to me, and the fish were there." Her throat sounded tight and pinched. "They handed me the fishbowl and the fish. They were floating in it, bloated and black and dead. I can still see them, floating next to a cinder. It was horrible," she shuddered. "So horrible."

TEN BOXES | 163

Like a game of KerPlunk, the little marbles of thought skipped and plinked and plunked all the way down through my years with her, all the way to now. Something was slowly making sense to me about her, in ways it hadn't before. I listened to how she called her mother "Mother," not "Mom." I watched how her body somehow became small – unprotected and raw and scared – when she was talking about her fish.

I felt awful. Criminal. Cruel. After all this, after days of work and dozens upon dozens of bags of stuff thrown away, I felt as though I'd done more harm than good.

I'd known about their house burning down, inasmuch as I'd been told that it happened. I don't remember her ever having told me the story in detail, and I certainly didn't remember ever having heard that the neighbors had stolen their stuff.

Now, heaping loss upon loss, so had I. No wonder she'd been sad for days. I'd stolen her stuff, her security blanket, her comfort, her home. No matter that there was more of it than there was of her. No matter that with an unexpected collapse she might be buried alive. She already was, somehow, years ago. And like Humpty Dumpty, all the EST training and all the gurus in the world couldn't quite put her together again. It's a hard lesson to learn, at 8 or 10, that homes *do* burn down, that sometimes no one is there to help you, and that you can't trust people who say they are helping. No wonder she never asked us for help.

Tears were rolling down my cheeks as we walked back to the car that night. (Yes, we'd cleaned that, too, by the way. It was Mom's project while I was working on part of the living room during Day Three of my stay. It was still dirty, but at least there was room for two people in the front seats now. And she *swore* that the boxes in the backseat would be taken to Goodwill that week, though I knew better. At this point, that was okay.) She apologized, again, this time for the fact that she'd made me sad. I just smiled. She had no idea. Up to that point in my life, it's possible that I'd never known the guilt of hurting someone deeply. I was a kind and thoughtful kid, and if I lost friends, it was due to distance, not distaste. I'd never had anyone "hate" me, never broken a heart, never thrown a punch. But now I knew that inside my mom was a black and blue and bloody mess, and I was the one who was so sorry, so sad.

She took me to the airport when I left the following day, having enough room in the car now to handle both my bag and me. We hugged tightly, spoke little, parted as though I'd never left home.

When I got back to Atlanta, we talked more often for a while, or, perhaps, spoke more freely. I asked frequently about the house, the car, how she was doing. She told me that things were fine, that she was keeping the house orderly, that the car was chugging along. I was too far away to know whether she was telling the truth, so I hoped for the best. I went on living my life, working, trying to figure out relationships and what I wanted to be someday, once I finally grew up.

I didn't get to Florida much. I sent Mom tickets to visit as often as I could, at least once a year. I found it easier that way. She didn't have to hide whatever state her home was in, and I could entertain her, show her the town, talk and enjoy her company without the distress of "stuff." Things were, finally, easy between us again.

CHAPTER 11

1997

By way of telling one tale, sometimes we must tell a second to flesh out the first. It is not *her* story, this one, as much as it is *ours*. It did not happen to her, but it affected everything she touched. The tale of my mom, of her hoarding, of our lives, cannot be told fully without the story of what happened next.

By the summer of 1997, Adam and I were whittling away our savings on airfare between Chicago and Atlanta, and it seemed that if we were to be together, some decision must be made. I was visiting him over the 4th of July holiday, and we spent a day at the edge of Lake Michigan exploring the sights, sounds, and smells of the annual "Taste of Chicago" festival. We'd used some tickets to take a Ferris wheel ride, and on our final go-round, as we sat at the apex with people loading and unloading below, I announced that I'd decided I would move to Chicago.

Adam was delighted. I was more innately adventurous than he was, and he was somewhat intimidated by the idea of leaving behind the familiar to set up house somewhere new. I'd already pretty much perfected the whole moving thing, so I was ready to take it on again. Leaving my friends in Atlanta was among the most difficult decisions of my life, and one that I'm not entirely certain I'd make again, if circumstances were the same. But that's why they say we live and learn.

I wasn't sure how I'd tackle the move, finding a job, making my way in a whole new city. Within a few months, it was all solved when the company for which we both worked posted a position at the home office, in Chicago. I flew up and interviewed, and I was chosen for the job within weeks. An October start date was set, and I began preparing and saying my long goodbyes.

I'd painted the living room of my bachelorette pad a deep plum (damson, Byzantium). My landlady had graciously agreed to my chosen paint scheme (rust and mustard in the bedroom, too) if I agreed that, upon moving out, I'd repaint back to a nice, neutral beige (eggshell, cream). I'd agreed with fervor, eager to have my very own place feel like my very own place. Come September of 1997, however, I regretted my style as I stood in the middle of my living room, staring at the daunting task ahead. It was unclear exactly how many coats of almost-white would be required to cover purple-nearly-black walls. It was obvious that the three coats I'd already applied were quite insufficient.

Covered in paint, I stood analyzing, and reached for the phone when it rang with my almost-clean left hand.

"Hey." It was Mom. "Hey" was never a great conversation starter coming from her.

"Hey."

"Are you still painting?"

"Yep. Maybe I will be all week. I don't know if I'll ever finish."

"Are you alone?"

"Yeah, right now. Robert was helping, and he's supposed to come back later."

"Can you sit down for a minute?"

"Huh?"

"I need to talk to you for a minute. Can you sit down?"

I did, though I was a little frustrated. I had open paint and wet rollers and brushes laying everywhere. I had paint on my hands, on my face, in my hair. I felt impatient, like I was back in grade school, waiting for her to finish sewing my hem, because I was going to be late – again.

"Your dad's been hurt."

"Oh, God."

I imagine there aren't many people alive who don't know the feeling: The feeling in your throat that rises up from your chest and then sinks down again, deep, settling in the pit of your stomach. The feeling of being chained to the tracks with a speeding train headed your way. You know you've only got seconds until everything will be different forever, and there's no goddamned way to move. The words are about to hit your ears, and you want to scream, "NONONONONONONONONO!" so that you cannot hear them.

Seconds before, I could not get through the conversation quickly enough, and suddenly I sat, begging the sounds to cease, midair, and hang there forever, undelivered. Breathing, gasping, I was swallowing air so the sounds could not travel through it.

"He's in the hospital, at Bayfront."

"What happened? Was he in an accident?"

"He was stabbed."

"What?"

"He was stabbed. I'm not sure exactly. He was driving the taxi. Some kid, I guess, stabbed him. I don't know."

"When? How did this . . .? When? Is he okay?"

"He's alive. It happened last night, really late. He was about to go off his shift. I guess it happened right after his last fare. It was late. By the time the hospital called Wilma, and Casey called me, it was too late to call you. I didn't want to wake you up, in case you wanted to come down, I wanted you to be rested. There was nothing you could do at 3 a.m."

Gulping, still. "Stabbed? Is he . . .? I mean . . . What . . .?"

"He was in surgery most of the night. He's up in CCU now. He was pretty bad."

I wasn't sure how much more I could process. I'd always been a believer in cause and effect: Good deeds lead to heaven. Bad deeds are punished. What you do comes back to you. Good things happen to good people. Karma. We are not meaningless and adrift. I'd held strong, through my frequently changing religious affiliation – or lack thereof – to the idea of some "grand design," some great equilibrium in the world. Just over a year before, I'd gotten my first tattoo – a yin/yang – to remind me of my belief in the presence, recognized or not, of a universal balance. In the moment, however, my carefully constructed personal spirituality dissolved into a sea of unknowing. Random violence can do that, and did do that, to me.

It was touch-and-go; none of us really knew what to do. I was supposed to be moving in two weeks. Most of my things were already packed. I wasn't sure whether to get on an airplane or into a car, whether to cancel my move and scrap the new job altogether. I was afraid that if I started driving right then, he could die before I got there, and I'd be on the road and would not know he was dead. (I had no cell phone in my life then. In '97, they weren't as mandatory as breathing.) If he died and I was driving, I would be, without knowing, speeding toward his corpse, which struck me as unbearably morbid. I still thought clocks should stop when people died, and all forward motion should cease.

But what if I *could* get there in time? Or what if he was going to be fine?

Feeling one foot nailed to the floor, I picked up my paintbrush and started painting my walls again – another coat. I was in shock. Of course, I wasn't aware of it until my friend Robert showed back up and couldn't reconcile the tears running down my cheeks with the task at hand. When I told him what had happened, he offered to finish painting for me. I told him he couldn't, because I could not stop. My ridiculously purple walls were, at that moment, my link to sanity.

So instead, he stayed all day and watched, and helped, and said nothing, except what was necessary. Hours later, he took the brush out of my hand when I started to drop it from fatigue, though the purple was still peeking out around corners from the white (ecru, nude). And finally, the next day, when Adam flew in from Chicago, and we climbed in my car to drive south, Robert finished painting the living room for me.

I lost track of Robert just a handful of days later. I don't know whether he was ever sufficiently thanked. I hope he's still around. He was kind, confused, and a mystery none of us had finished solving.

As my living room was being painted in Atlanta, the drive to St. Pete was one of the longest of my life. I refused to let Adam drive, certain that the steering wheel was as apt a pacifier as any paintbrush. We were mostly silent. I sped. Somewhere around Gainesville, I got pulled over. It's amazing how far the truth can go. The kind officer let me pull away, citation-free, when I told him my father had been stabbed and was in the hospital. His parting words were, "Well, then, you'd better slow down. He don't need you in the hospital, too." Point taken, I set the cruise control.

The three days spent in St Pete are still a blur. Dad was still in the Critical Care Unit, so only one or two people could visit at a time. Visiting hours were supposed to be limited, but the nurses did what they could to allow us in as much as possible, given the circumstances. Dad was wheeled into surgery again and out again, and we came and went, holding his hand, talking to him in his unconsciousness.

Detectives came and went.

Counselors came and went.

More detectives. More counselors.

More doctors.

And Dad held on, his condition roller-coastering.

Detectives found the boy who had stabbed Dad. I was with my mom when they explained what was happening. I remember looking at one of them, Detective Shakas, and thinking that he was working as hard as the doctors and nurses were. Everyone seemed so sincere, so invested in helping my dad. I just wanted to keep thanking them all for being so nice to us. It was all the attention they could give us, even if the reason was a horrible one.

"He's eighteen," the detective said, "so he'll be tried as an adult, no question. Right now, we're looking at assault, assault with a deadly weapon likely. Robbery. If, uh, your dad should, um –" He shuffled his feet, adjusted the radio at his hip. "If his condition worsens, God forbid, and he should pass, then the charge converts to murder."

It sat heavy. Murder. Where was I? These things don't happen to my family. How had we ended up here, and what was going on?

"You should know, miss," they said to me, "your father was very brave. He's a fighter. We have a lot of evidence, from the car. The nurses. He, um, he was smart, your dad. I don't know how long it would've taken EMS to get there, but the nurses said he drove himself to the hospital here. He was smart enough to get over here fast, not wait for the ambulance. He didn't have a lot of time. I'm sorry, I know this is difficult."

Difficult was not the word for what we were hearing. There are special rooms in hospitals for hearing words like these. Most people never have to see those quiet rooms where words like "murder" are spoken.

"The ER staff will be good witnesses. They saw him pull up, get out, and slide down the side of his cab. He was losing a lot of blood. He knew it, though, we think that's why he drove himself. The cab – it's bad. The ER nurses rushed out while he was still conscious."

I could not help but think of the bleeding wounds. I could not help but imagine crimson streaks on a sunshine yellow cab. And then I could not stop thinking of my dad, begging a boy, over and over, to stop stabbing him. I could not stop imagining him, alone in a taxi, racing for help. I could not hear anything but the pulse in my ears until I heard, ". . . the fare from Tony's Meat Market."

"Where?" I asked.

"Tony's Meat Market. Apparently it's where your dad picked up his last fare. He was able to tell the nurses, as they wheeled him into surgery, that 'the kid I picked up at Tony's Meat Market' had done it."

"Did that help you find him?"

"Yes. That and the photo."

They told us Dad also picked the kid out of a photo lineup. They told us that they might never have found the kid if it weren't for my dad. What they did not – could not – tell me was whether my father would live.

Days later, when it seemed there was nothing to do but wait, I decided to go ahead with my planned move to Chicago. We hoped that Dad would be alright, would heal, would recover. I knew he was happy for me, for my new relationship, and he wanted to see me loved and in love, so I knew what was best was to keep on keeping on. I prayed every day that my stamina would cosmically recharge his spirit.

I forfeited my security deposit when I moved because my bedroom was still rust and mustard.

Eleven weeks, three visits back to Florida, and umpteen surgeries for my dad later, the phone rang on the desk at my new job in my new city.

Mom told me that if I wanted to come down, it was time to visit Dad again, one last time, because this was the end.

I flew to Florida the next day.

The doctors' valiant efforts and nurses' diligent care were as useful, in the end, as the storied "all the king's horses and all the king's men," and they could not put my father back together again. The stabbing had been done with a serrated kitchen knife, like a steak knife. The wounds were jagged, the sepsis was hearty, and every good hour was followed by several bad ones. The years of prescription drug abuse, I imagined, hadn't helped the situation. Eventually, Dad's major organs had begun to shut down.

The doctors said that he was brain dead by the time I arrived, that the ventilator was pretty much the only thing keeping him alive. I didn't believe it then, nor to this day have I been able to embrace it. He was flat on his back, staring at the ceiling, so I climbed onto a stool to get into his line of sight. And I talked to him. I told him how much I loved him, and how much I appreciated him being my dad.

Tears rolled down his cheeks. And I sang to him –
and sang, and sang, very quietly, and in broken
tones – every song I could think of, every hymn I
knew words for. I sang until everyone else arrived,
and until my mom came into the room to say that it
was time. She rested one hand on my shoulder, and
one hand on top of my hand that was holding my
father's, and I began to tremble.

The gathering for his departure was, at best,
complete. Jonelle was there, mother to all of his
children and his wife of 21 years. Wilma, my
stepmother, was there, too. My brothers both stood
in the circle around the bed, next to Uncle Charlie,
Aunt Becky, and Aunt Linda. We all stood close. We
all held tight, as the nurse and the morphine eased
my father into deeper and deeper unconsciousness.
Until his heartbeat stopped. Until all of the pain, the
love, the hurt, the longing, the unspoken words that
get strewn across years and lost into time's
quicksand were finished, all at once, with the
nurse's whisper, "He's gone."

It's policy, it seems, to ask the family to leave the
room at this point. Turning off a ventilator isn't
always pretty: Muscles contract, air escapes, and to
a fragile mourner, the dead may seem to gasp or
moan, reanimated. I was steeled for the moment,
but the hospital staff insisted it was "best."

When they were finished, my mom asked if I
wanted to go back in and see him. I wasn't sure, but
I went. What I saw lives on in me: My father was

gone. Absolutely gone. There was this body lying in a bed, and it was a body that looked a lot like his. But he was gone, light-years away. The room had grown cold. Like an abandoned house, the vast emptiness of the place was palpable.

It was then, in that void, that I remembered that I was truly not alone in my grief. I turned to see my mom standing there, nose red, hands full of wadded up Kleenex and sorrow. I realized that she was alone now. They'd divorced years before for too many reasons, but had managed over time to be friendly. As I looked at her, I saw all of their shared memories playing across her face. She had never remarried and never would. My father had been her one grand adventure into an attempt at lasting love, and now she would bear the memories alone, a forever eulogy reciting itself for him again and again.

After the memorial service, back in his childhood hometown of Frostproof, we gathered at the clubhouse near the mobile home he and Wilma had moved into a few years before. When eating and drinking and chatter had slowed to a halt, and the day was winding down into the saddest sunset, Wilma asked whether we (my brothers, my mom, and I) wanted any of Dad's things.

I stood frozen in their room, at his dresser, near his closet. I didn't know where to start, or what to keep, or how one builds a memory. I didn't know what my heart might someday find comforting. So my mother helped me. Because she understood *stuff*. She knew that a flannel shirt, and his old corduroy jacket, replete with pocket flaps and elbow patches, would be just the things to slip on and sit in when I missed him the most.

I thought then, standing in my father's bedroom holding corduroy, flannel, denim, about how long she'd kept the last piece of their wedding cake in the freezer. And the jars of wine jelly that had been wedding gifts, which sat, unopened, forever in our china cabinet. And the little bottle of sand they'd brought back from Nassau, collected during their honeymoon. And the dressy Seiko watch he bought for her, the one she never wore.

I wondered if all the stuff, or any of it, would help us hold on to him just a little longer.

CHAPTER 12

Betrayal

bout two years later, Joan decided to sell her property and the house Mom lived in, so my mom had to move. I wish I knew now what I was doing then: I was "busy." Probably back in school, studying for the next of my now several careers. I didn't go to Florida to help. Maybe I didn't even want to. I certainly had no skills to deal with more triage, so perhaps I stayed away to keep the peace and keep my sanity.

She'd found a place, she told me, down on the south side of town but near the water. Being near the water had always been a curative for her. She'd told me that it was part of a duplex. It was a one-bedroom apartment, but it had a large living room, and the bedroom was more than enough space. It had a yard for gardening, was safe and affordable, and she said she felt good there. That was enough for me. I didn't see the place until she'd been there awhile.

I don't recall why I made my next trip home. It could be that I was already engaged to Adam and was excited and busily planning a wedding. It could be that it was Spring, and I had time and money enough to travel. It may have been for her birthday, perhaps her 60th. I don't recall enough of the details, just that I went, and that I saw her new home.

I stayed with my aunt Linda again, this time because Mom only had one bed. That seemed like a bullshit excuse. She was my mother, so we'd slept in the same bed on countless occasions on trips, in hotel rooms, and at friends' homes. There seemed to be no reason to break with the traditions brought on by necessity, but I was staying with my aunt nonetheless. My mom came over, of course, and we spent a great deal of time together. While we were out for a movie one afternoon, she said, "I just need to stop by my house." I was happy to have a chance to see it.

From the outside, it was clearly my mother's home. Her garden thrived, greenery taking over every formerly dank corner. Staghorn fern hung from the trees. Volunteer squash and watermelon vines made their way along fences, interwoven with black-eyed-Susans (which she said she'd grown for me) and foxglove. It was a little corner of Eden and just as perfect.

I was nervous as she opened her front door. "Careful," she cautioned, "don't let the cats out." How many? I wondered. But as we stepped inside, I took heart.

Her new place was crowded – that was a given in my mind before entering, and I knew there would be piles of stuff. But as I stepped through the door, I saw sunlight coming through the blinds. There *were* piles, but not too, too many. There was stuff, to be sure, but you could navigate around it without trouble. There were seats to sit on with no stuff in them. The couch was bare except for throw pillows. The bedroom was overcrowded a bit, but her bed was obviously for sleeping, and she could get in and out of it with little interference, except for what might come from the nine cats.

Stop. What?

Yes, nine. And yes, the bathroom smelled of urine, and I could not be certain whether that was from the three litter boxes in the hall or from my mother. I'd seen much worse, so by comparison, I was relieved. I'd become fairly certain that perhaps the worst was over, that maybe together we'd somehow exorcised a few of her demons. I failed to recognize the cyclical nature of her disease, and thought somehow this reprieve meant she'd ascended out of her madness. I suppose even Newton might have lent a hand, for as with gravity, it was also with my mother's mettle. What goes up must come down.

For the next couple of years, I allowed myself to believe what I was told. My brother, Carl, had come back to town and was living not too far from Mom. He'd been in Seattle a long time, but had split from his wife Theresa and had long endured her refusing him access to their kids.

It was hard for him to fight for guardianship. He wasn't a good role model. Carl had struggled with finding and keeping employment that fulfilled him. He was smart; he was always busy figuring out how to one-up "the system," and several times he ended up in trouble with the law as a result. Carl also was a born horticulturist, and his ability to produce bounty manifested in many kinds of crops, including those still illegal in most states at the time. He also struggled, I believe, with his own mental illness. I'd heard him talk about bouts of depression, and had been told that while in Seattle he'd experienced the kind of deep paranoia that I'd come to recognize as hyper-mania.

When he moved back to St. Pete, Carl told Mom that he was resigned that Theresa would never let him near the kids. He tried starting over and met someone new, a nurse who Mom said he seemed crazy about. Head-over-heels, she'd said. Carl lost her when she was killed in a car wreck that they endured together, but only he survived. I remember that Mom said she drove a Corvette. When I see them now, speeding down the interstate, I still think about the dead nurse whose name I don't remember. I wish she had lived. I always want to know the alternate ending to a story.

Once Carl started to recover from her loss, he started over yet again with Rachel, a new wife and another child, a baby boy. (I never really knew what to call Carl's wives, because I did not know whether they were ever legally married. There were never family weddings or large celebrations, and I don't know whether they ever even visited the courthouse. They lived as husbands and wives do, so I called them wives. It was simple, when little else could be easily explained.)

Sometime in the early '90s, Theresa appeared at Carl and Rachel's door, with three children in tow. Carl might not have known them, save family resemblance, because it had been so long since he'd seen his own kids. The two boys were already in high school, and his daughter was soon to be. Theresa announced that she was having some struggles with her mental health, and she was leaving the kids with Carl - they were now suddenly his responsibility. He was completely unprepared, but having been forced away from them for more than a decade, he was delighted with the challenge.

Having the kids back seemed like a gift to the whole family, and they seemed to make Mom, especially, feel truly happy and – as children of any age had always seemed to – purposeful. There were mysteries of life to be explored, *adventures* to go on, things to teach, and things to learn. There were small joys like art projects shared with Grandma that led to Mom's larger joys of knowing her kin, hearing her own heartbeat echoed in theirs. I heard mostly happy stories from Mom of afternoons spent with the kids, sharing the places and things that their father had loved as a youngster. Carl and Rachel continued to have financial struggles, as they seem to be a part of my family's genetic code, but beyond that, life was a rich pageant, and my mom seemed, for a while, to be enjoying the show.

Still, Carl was hoeing a tough row. As his children descended upon their household, Rachel - who Mom had said was "nuts" from the moment she'd met her - became more and more unstable. Carl woke one night to find her trying to push a 30-gallon aquarium over and onto him. He said Rachel had told him several times that she was going to kill him, and he began to feel unsafe with her in the house, especially around his kids. Ultimately, to protect his sanity as well as his children, he asked the court to place a restraining order on her, which it did.

So he was left to raise his kids alone. The task became easier after the first few months, when his eldest son left to begin his military career, and soon after, the next eldest boy left, following a path into the merchant marines. Life was slightly simpler then, with only two children – a teenage girl from one wife and a boy from another – remaining in his charge, but he was still struggling. Our mom and my other brother, Casey, did what they could to help. They stayed with the kids when necessary and pulled together to try to help Carl pull through. But slowly, all of this pulling began to pull at my mom's strings, the ones that held her delicately together.

Again, now, it seemed she was "on the go" more often than not. She was still working some, off the books here and there, to make ends meet. She was entertaining grandchildren, trying to help their father keep their home clean, trying to teach them things that their mothers hadn't. She was trying to instill years' worth of her grandmotherly love into them, quickly, condensed but without abbreviation.

Rachel made casual reappearances at Carl's home, letting herself in (read: breaking in) on a couple of occasions. For several weeks, she slept in a tent in his back yard. He allowed it, taking pity on her and knowing she had no relatives near, and nowhere, really, to go. When she finally became confrontational again, he reminded her of the restraining order and asked her to leave. She refused repeatedly, so finally, at the end of his proverbial rope, he called the police.

If you don't live a terribly legal existence, calling the police can sometimes backfire. It did.

As the police were dragging Rachel away from Carl's home, she said to them, "I don't know why you're arresting *me*. *He's* the one growing pot in his basement."

And so it was that the light of probable cause came to shine on the threshold of my brother's home. And lo, it did come to pass that Carl was arrested.

So, now my brother's in jail, and these two kids are parentless. Initially, it was thought that my brother would be through the court system quickly. Social workers decided, with the cooperation of my mom and my other brother, that the family would work together to provide care for Carl's children until his case had been tried. Mom and Casey did their best, pooling resources of both time and money, making do and running kids to school and back between work and life. My mom tried to make their lives as normal as possible, insisting that they stay in their own home and out of "the system." She slept there with them some nights, with Casey staying there other nights. She never slept well in that house, though; she said the house felt "strange."

I was told something a long time ago that I still believe to be true: A child from a home where there is infidelity becomes incredibly sensitive to issues around fidelity, develops a sort of sixth sense about it. The same can be said of a child raised in a sexually abusive environment. Children are intuitive, observant, sensitive creatures. They learn unspoken subtleties without being taught. My mom had this kind of sixth sense, as do I, about fidelity. I knew what she meant when she said, "I just know."

I also know what it feels like to know a thing – a thing you are not ready to confront – and how quickly it can drive your thoughts into bedlam.

After Carl had been in jail for a few weeks, with constantly shifting possibilities for freedom, Mom called me one night. She asked me things she didn't usually ask, like whether I had time to talk, if I was busy, and whether I was sure we could talk because she needed to. I knew something was deeply wrong, not only from the questions, but from her haunted – even frightened – tone of voice.

It sounded like cancer.

It sounded like her house had burned down again, stealing everything away with the flames.

It sounded like someone was dying, and in a way, I suppose she was.

Mom started the conversation by telling me how the kids were, and what they'd all been doing together. Then she talked about Carl's house, telling me that it felt strange, that she could never really relax, that she got a "funny" feeling when she was there. While the kids were at school, she'd been spending some time trying to make the place orderly and keeping it as clean and as "homey" as she could, she said.

Allow me to interject here that if my mother was "cleaning house," and you happened to be a child in said house, your personal privacy was not her number one concern. In fact, your privacy was not a concern to her *at all* if your well-being was in question; I could provide several firsthand accounts of my experiences with this.

Mom told me that she'd been cleaning Carl's place earlier that day, and was putting laundry away in her granddaughter's room when she found something that concerned her. There was lingerie in the closet and in a drawer that seemed terribly inappropriate for a 16-year-old who had already told my mom that she didn't have a boyfriend. With her sensitivities in full swing and her protective urges swelling up, Mom began to investigate, poking around in drawers, in books, on shelves. She looked for what she already knew was there until she found it.

She found letters – from her own son to his own daughter. Letters not from a father to a child, but from a man to a woman. Intimate letters, penned by a hand that she knew too well, extolling love and kindred spirits, pronouncing her beauty and his lust. There it was, on paper before her, and all she could do was shake and cry. She left the house before the kids came home from school and asked Casey to stay with them that night. She went home and wept and wept and wept until she was finally able to call me.

We talked every day in the following weeks. She wrestled with her conscience. She sat sleepless with her son's guilt and his progeny's future perched in her lap. She was uncertain, some days, whether it would be worse for him to return to the home and the children, or worse for the children to be thrown, willy-nilly, into what she already recognized was a weak and floundering foster care system. She didn't know how to address the matter with her granddaughter, and whether or not the girl would lie. Mom didn't want her to feel ashamed or at fault, but she also didn't want her to believe that what was happening was right. Mom wrestled every day – stomach churning and blood pressure skyrocketing – with what decision to make.

Finally, she called the kids' caseworker and told what she'd found. I cannot imagine the feeling that lived in her heart from that day forward. She did the only thing that was right, but betrayed her flesh and blood in the process, and tore two children's home asunder. She worried - was her action the lesser of two evils? I don't know if she ever convinced herself that it was.

My brother was charged, and ultimately convicted, for having ongoing sexual relations with his child. His daughter, though admitting what had happened, refused to consider the relationship abusive, as she had become convinced that they were "soul mates." She was a very smart young lady, but she could not be convinced that she'd been taken advantage of in any way.

Carl did not admit to any wrongdoing, as he "barely knew her" as his child, but had come to know her as a blossoming, beautiful young woman when she was brought to his house as a teenager. Their denial only hurt my mom further, shaking her confidence in her decision.

My brother was given 20 years in prison. Both kids ended up in foster care – one until she graduated and ventured, waif-like, into the world, the other until grandparents far away claimed him as their own and did what they could to return his life to some semblance of normalcy.

In the months following the heartache, Mom reeled. Being a whistleblower is never easy, even when it's done for the best reasons, even with the most impenetrable proof, and especially not when the culprit is your flesh, your blood, your bones. She believed she'd created a monster, somehow, and day after day, she sought to figure out where she'd erred. She was both Frankenstein and the frightened villagers, and there seemed to be no way out of the paradox.

Every abuser, every unwanted advance, every wrong touch from her childhood returned to menace her daily, so her thoughts spun out of control. Then and now became as inseparable, and as sad, as a care package of poems forever soiled with melted candle wax.

I talked with her as often as I could then, in the following, deeply saddening days. I tried to call daily, or nearly so. I could tell that she wasn't well, although she tried to sound as if she was. I checked in with Casey and with my aunt. I worried every time Mom didn't return my calls, and went sleepless when she hadn't called back after days and days.

I was nearly always prepared for bad news concerning her, her health, her whereabouts. Because I knew she'd talked about it in the past, some days, I steeled myself for news of her suicide, though I believed in my heart of hearts that she was stronger than that. I'd been depressed in my life, but the depth of her sadness then was one I could not – will not ever – know completely.

CHAPTER 13

Observation

After about a year, I'd thought that Mom might begin a process of recovery. Always the optimist (for little reason), I thought somehow the weight of Carl's sins would shift, and Mom would be able to breathe again. Instead, I got a call from Casey: the middle child, a quiet underdog, stronger than any of us knew, and absolutely capable of pulling his shit together when we least expected it.

Casey was calling to talk to me about our mom. Time had not yet healed her wounds, and she was clearly not only in deep pain but in terrible mental distress. I blamed Carl, and I felt like Casey did, too, though we never said so. After all our mom had lived through, and all of the children she had championed, it was one of them that in the end had broken her indefatigable heart.

"I hate to have to call you about this," Casey said, "I know it's upsetting, and you're kind of far away."

"No, it's okay. Just – what's going on?"

"Well, I've been talking with Linda, and we're real worried about Mom right now. She's real unstable."

"What's going on? Is she depressed again? Is that why she hasn't called me back in a few days? Did she lose her duplex?!"

"No, well – no. That's the thing. We're not exaaaactly sure what's up there. The neighbors say she's come and gone recently. But she never opens the door if her car is there. We think she doesn't want us inside."

"Why?"

"Well, now – you know how Mom is. And the house is full of stuff. Like the last time she even cracked the door for me was months ago, but that day I could see right past her, all the piles of –"

"Yeah," I sympathized. "Everything. Stuff."

"It's just that she's starting to not make sense, and I'm afraid she's gonna get pulled over. Her car isn't tagged, and she's still driving it. She isn't driving well, I should add."

"Casey, how is this different? I mean, I want to help, but . . .?"

"Well, Linda and I are kind of worried because she even looks like she's not taking care of herself. We think she's real, real manic right now, Sue. The last time I talked to her, she said something about not sleeping for a couple of days."

"Shit."

"Yeah. I hate to say it, but it's pretty hardcore, sister. Mom's been driving around in her car, like day and night. She sleeps in it sometimes. And I've seen her parked at the Northeast Shopping Center, taking notes. She carries these spiral notebooks everywhere now, and always notes things."

"Like she's having memory trouble?"

"No. Like the license plate of every single car that parked on her street. Or that parked in front of Publix on Tuesday. Or that drove past her at the stoplight. It's kind of crazy stuff. And when Linda saw her, and the last time I saw her – she rambles a lot, Sue. But she's been dodging everybody. And I know she isn't taking care of her health, and with diabetes, it makes me wonder if it's affecting her eyes, which may be why she drives like she can't see the road half the time."

"Christ."

"We've tried to talk to her, but she just gets paranoid. She thinks everybody's watching her. She needs to sleep; she won't listen to reason. I'm really worried. Her place is so bad that if the neighbors know, they might call the city. I'm surprised the landlord hasn't already."

I sighed. "She won't go see anyone, will she?"

"That would be reasonable. She's not into reasonable right now."

"And Linda and Becky?

"They say the same thing. Please, call them if you want to. I don't want you to feel pushed into anything. She needs to be on some meds, though, Sue. Soon. It's bad. I just don't know what else to do but have her taken in for observation."

I sighed. I knew it was coming, but now it had come. That word: "observation." Like a fungus in a petri dish, fish in an aquarium, prisoners in a cell. But if it were a choice between living in an aquarium or being dead on the street, I knew my preference.

"I want her safe," I said.

"Me too. That's why I called. I just – I won't do it without you saying you're okay with it. And then there's the house . . ."

"Okay. I'm with you. Do what you need to do. I'm on my way. I'll leave really early tomorrow and be down by afternoon. But if it can't wait –"

"I think we'd better call the authorities."

"Police or . . . ?"

"I think so. I think it's St. Pete P.D., but it might be a Pinellas County Sherriff thing. I can call and figure it out."

It was hard to believe that in order to get her help we had to, essentially, have her arrested. But I knew it was true. I sighed. "Ok. Thanks. Jesus . . ."

"I'm just worried, you know." Casey paused. "I'm worried she'll get hurt. Or hurt somebody, cause an accident –"

"I get it. Thanks, Casey. I'm sorry."

"Yeah, me too. Fuck."

"Yeah. Fuck."

"Talk to you soon, drive safe," he said, and we hung up.

I'd started a business with a friend about a year prior and was able to work from almost anywhere. (The irony was never lost on me that we ran a skip tracing agency, and spent our days working to collect on defaulted auto loans.) My partner didn't hesitate when I said that I was needed out of town.

I wasn't present for Mom's detention, which occurred the same day that I arrived, but earlier. It was, apparently, quite a scene. Not in her right mind, scared, sure that we were all out to get her, my poor mom resisted the police officers who'd come to "escort" her to her psychiatric evaluation, and then ran from them. When they caught her by the arm, she continued to resist, dropping her considerable full weight to her hands and knees. She hollered. She screamed. She had to be dragged to her feet several times. She had to be handcuffed. She pled with the police; she pled to God and to my brother. She cut herself at one point when she fell. It was, I can only imagine, a bloody, frightening mess.

By the time I got to St. Pete, the family had begun to gather. My aunts, Becky and Linda, were there, as was Casey, and another set of helping hands, Linda C., who was a friend of my aunt's and had been good to our whole family for almost as long as I could remember. Mom had been taken to a mental health facility for evaluation, and she would spend a minimum of 72 hours under observation. We'd be able to see her after 24. Meanwhile, her abode sat in wait for us. We talked, planned, and consoled each other as we steeled our nerves to head over to see what had become of her home.

There is no way to prepare for days like that one and the days that followed. Five days, all told, with five people working, sunup to sundown. Five days of digging through massive piles of junk and jewels, relics and rubbish.

The first thing that became apparent, upon entering the house, was that it was worse than any of her homes had ever been. The cloying sting of urine hit our faces the moment the front door was shoved open, against resistance from the pile of stuff toppled over behind it. From the threshold, there was barely a path. If we looked carefully, we could see the spaces where the piles weren't as high and were less likely to slide, which seemed to be the obstacle course that Mom had been navigating in order to get into the house. It was kind of like a tire course, where you have to step wide left and then wide right, hoping not to fall on your ass in the mud – or, in this case, into a pile of shit. Literally: There was cat shit everywhere.

The living room I'd seen just three years before, which was so uncluttered and open-feeling, was now a den of paper. There were the usual suspects – books, magazines, clippings – but now there were more of them, and they were less well cared for.

Books had always been nearly sacred to my mom. Even in her messiest houses, the books were on shelves. They might have been stacked three deep, lying on their sides, or, if she were desperate, they might have sat on the floor for a few days, but she'd have placed them there ever so carefully. She had always had a reverence for the printed word, which now seemed to have slipped away. Books had fallen, slid, and piled up sideways and diagonally and upside down. Things had been spilled on magazines, and they'd stuck together, their pages now inseparable and unreadable, but still lying in the pile.

Lamps, some of them valuable antiques, were on their sides underneath clothing and boxes and wind chimes and old photographs. I could not rest my eyes on a square foot of space without wondering what in the hell all of the things occupying that space had in common. Here I was again, singing "One of These Things is Not Like the Other," but this time I sang it aloud. Aunt Becky, a schoolteacher who got the reference, laughed. Then Casey laughed, and then we all laughed for a very long time, because we could not cry.

We *wanted* to cry. My mom was no longer using her bedroom. She was sleeping, instead, in the kitchen, or so it seemed. A twin-size mattress was laid in the middle of her tiny kitchen floor: no box spring, no sheet. One very old pillow, barely holding its form, looked more like a softening potato than a pillow. There was no room to walk around or past the mattress – it filled the entire floor – and on it was more cat shit. All around the mattress, piled on every inch of kitchen counter space, was more stuff, all the way to the back door, which could not be opened for the stuff blocking it.

The bedroom had surrendered to the stuff many weeks – perhaps even months – before. The piles had slid and fallen over so that the door could not be pushed in. My mom, not as strong as she'd once been, had probably simply given up trying before she resolved to sleep in the kitchen. The odor of congealed urine and dander were so thick in the air – and on nearly every surface – that we all hacked and sneezed and coughed, wondering whether we might also be inhaling some lethal microbe or other.

My mother's home – a place that once welcomed guests, cared for children, nursed the infirm, gave comfort to the lonely – was now only one step above the city dump, and the only reason for that ranking was because we loved her.

We had a dumpster at our disposal. It seemed barely big enough. The top layer of everything was trash. It had not always been so, but the stench, the shit, the piss, the fur, the dander, and the rancor of her sadness and her loss clung to every surface with unwashable certainty. Box after box, heavy-duty lawn bag after bag after bag, 33 gallons at a time, we simply hauled it out. Every so often one of us would stop to pause, to breathe, to drink water, or to cherish something that we'd found intact: A small black sheep from our childhood manger, still on Mom's shelf, under so much weight, tucked away. A picture of her, young and smiling. A gift given to her by one of us, made by childhood hands. But these were the diamonds, and we were mining, long hard days to find anything of beauty that remained lost in the mire.

I found – and kept for a very, very long time – several of her spiral bound notebooks of ramblings from the weeks prior to her commitment. Every page was scrawled, front and back, with words and numbers and license plate combinations. There were shopping lists and schemes and names of people she thought were after her. Lists of people she thought owed her money. Notes on important places she needed to go, plans she needed to complete, people she needed to help, or feed, or take care of.

The notes reminded me of George, one of the sweetest men I've ever known, who was a patient of my mom's when I was a teenager. George was schizophrenic and mostly deaf, and he had shown me his notebooks, which were filled with formulas and words and numbers, like my mother's.

I was afraid, for her and for myself. I'd never seen notebooks like these, except George's, and now my mom's. I was afraid that what had been overlooked for so long, then was diagnosed as bipolar disorder, was actually now schizophrenia. I was afraid she was even worse than we knew. For a very long time, I needed the notebooks as proof that we'd not done something foolish by placing her under observation. I needed the evidence of her madness so that my heart did not – would not, could not – convince me I'd gone awry in my own thoughts. I was afraid that if she was having trouble making decisions, maybe my genes were corrupted, and I was a poor decision-maker, too. I needed proof that my own mind had been sound when I agreed to commit my mom. I wanted proof that she really could not have cared for the 12 or 14 cats we figured had been living there.

The cats. We tried to trap them all, to coax them, but we lost a few when they sprinted away at high speeds. How could we rehome the 11 cats we caught? That day, the only way possible was to take them straight to the Humane Society, and my heart ached. They were just shy of wild, some of them, but they were hers, and she loved them all. The same way she loved every scrap of junk that started out a treasure.

From time to time, there would be a snicker from one of us that would build into a peal of laughter. We found things so incongruous that the absurdity was unforgettable:

"You will be coming into great wealth," straight from a fortune cookie, taped to an antique hand mirror that lay broken on the floor – under 17 other layers, mind you, but there it was.

A magazine, *The Utne Reader*, was my very favorite discovery. A publication that I knew well, it caught my eye amidst one of the shortest stacks, where it lay like a stepping stone. Mom and I had both shared a love for it. But it wasn't that it was that particular magazine that made me howl. It was the cover. There in type so large that it ate the page, lay the question: "Stuff: Can We Escape?" I tittered, then guffawed, and then roared and roared and roared as I stood there, holding the perfect question inside of the truest answer I'd ever seen. Then I cried as I kept laughing, until my sides hurt, until I just couldn't laugh again.

We kept what we could, or what we thought she'd need: clothes, a few dishes, a few of her longtime favorite trinkets that remained unbroken, a couple of lamps, linens – the ones that could be washed clean. We gave away what seemed reasonable: pots and pans, books that didn't make us retch from the smell. But most of it we hauled out and simply threw away. We'd have burned it on a pyre in the bay if we could: the great sadness, the great cleansing, the death of the mountain of shit.

I just now noticed that I've written about her stuff again. There was Mom, under observation, and I am busy still observing her stuff. Stuff is easy to describe. Her rage is so much more difficult. And not funny. And very much the ugly part I don't want to write.

When we were finally allowed to see her, she'd been sedated. I know that she was on meds when she was released from the hospital, but this many years later, I can't tell you which ones: Prozac, Zoloft, antipsychotics, maybe. Regardless, the first time I laid eyes on her at the hospital, she looked . . . old. She looked hollow, like her skin and bones were loose and empty, and her spirit was frozen somewhere far away. She looked furious, and her eyes were as black as they'd ever been and round. She would not hug me. She scowled. She was cold. Hard. She didn't want to talk, or the meds wouldn't let her. She didn't want anything much, at that point. She was raw and cold and just a little dead. She didn't know why we'd done what we'd done. She wanted to go home. She wanted her things. She wanted her cats. She wanted everything that was gone, including her trust in her children. She knew in her heart what had happened to everything, long before we told her. She probably even knew she'd never again own a cat. We were beyond cruel. She wanted, clearly, to be disowned by people that would own her in this way.

It was sad and lonely and the hardest thing I've met. She looked as though she'd gone entirely mad.

I stayed as long as I could. Anna was amazing and understanding back in our office in Atlanta. She willingly shouldered much of the work while I was away. Still, after Mom's house was cleaned out, mostly, and her release from the hospital was still pending "stabilization," I finally went back home, to my life, which fit like a cheap suit because my mom was not alright. The doctors only ever called it an "acute manic episode," but when I'd seen her at the hospital, I remember thinking that somewhere inside my mother was the darkest night anyone could survive.

CHAPTER 14

After

Mom wasn't locked away forever; this story doesn't get to be simple. As we'd hoped, she was stabilized and released about a week later. The meds knocked her out. There were a lot of meds, a lot of doctor visits, then different meds, different doctors. She slept. A lot.

She couldn't go back to the place she'd lived, and we'd had her condemnable car towed away. Aunt Linda opened her door, as she always has to the strays and the left-behind. She gave Mom a room and meals, transportation, and someone who cared. It wasn't easy; it could not have been. They loved each other very much, no doubt, but they had always been so very different. But those things, we learn, don't matter in the darkest days. When a roof and a meal and a hand is what we have, that is what we give. We push and pull and cheer and scream and chant and urge each other forward in the wonderful, terrible race. We don't think too much about the finish line. It's too far away.

I spoke with Mom often, and when she was asleep or outside, I'd try to have quick check-ins with Linda to see if Mom was alright. Was she taking her meds? Sleeping? Eating? Super-depressed? Does she shower?

Eventually, Mom got better, mostly. By sometime around 2002, she needed a place of her own, and somehow, with Linda's help and that of a couple of social workers who must have known what they were doing, she got her own small apartment in a building for seniors. I think that was hard for her to swallow – a senior facility – but she *was* over 60. There was a check-in system, so they knew if a resident hadn't been up and about for a day or two. It offered a distant, watchful eye and a ready hand if it was needed. We all felt pretty good about her being there.

Her apartment was a one-bedroom, but it was comfortable. Her kitchen was complete, and her bathroom had both tub and shower and was clean and tidy. She had comfortable secondhand furniture, the lamps we'd saved, and enough room for her favorite trinkets that had been salvaged from the wreck of her home. There were windows in the bedroom as well as the living room, though from the couch, she could see neighbors pass by on the breezeway, and privacy prevented opening the curtains wide there.

It was enough space. Enough. But as with stuff – and food or pills or booze, pick your poison – my family has a long history of having a little trouble comprehending the word "enough." She always felt just a little cramped there, She had grown up in houses, raised us in houses. Her last home, the duplex, felt tight because it shared a wall with a neighbor. But this? Neighbors all around. She could never quite breathe as easily. There was no garden.

Meanwhile, I'd married Adam in 2001, against my instincts and a bevy of complications. Within two years, the marriage had fallen apart, so I moved out and was living alone, stretching my wings. My days were spent, in nearly every way, to my taste again. Both my rented condo and my life were shabby-chic but divinely mine – entirely welcoming and comfortable.

I met a guy. Okay, I met a couple. But then I met *him*: William. My guy. My one and only from the night we met. I was madly in love, and to top it all off, money was loose. Looser than it had ever been in my life. My business was prospering; Anna and I were supportive of each other, happy, and bringing home pretty spectacular paychecks. I took a couple of expensive vacations, lost some weight, bought a little "stuff" for myself and my home. I finally decided that I could afford a new car, and instead of trading in my Civic, I offered it to my mom. I hoped it would let her stretch a bit, too, away from her tiny apartment. I bought a new car, another Honda.

I don't particularly believe in fate or destiny, but to this day, a tiny part of me wonders if I *had* to give her that car. Oh, for a while it was good. She could drive herself to all of the places she wanted and liked to go: the library, where she could sit, again surrounded by stacks of books; the lake, where she could feed the ducks; the beach, especially at sundown, to walk in the sand, or, if it was too cold, just to sit in the car and watch the little yellow dot fade to nothing at the horizon. If she was lucky, she'd see dolphins at the beach, or farm ducks (the big white ones) at the lake, or maybe find a new Anne Tyler book at the library, or see someone she knew, like Mrs. Tucker, whose kids had been raised with hers. Though by then, I'm not sure how much Mom liked that kind of chance encounter. Her trials showed in deep furrows on her face, and her hair was more silver, thinner than ever. I tried to encourage her to go ahead and "wash that gray right out of her hair," but it was still too much bother, the vanity thing.

She went to Catholic churches sometimes, because she still found comfort in the ceremony. She attended a couple of social gatherings of friends and like-minded "thinkers" from time to time, but her attendance had slowed since the worst of her troubles began. There was this reason or that not to attend, and some folks had moved on, but I still think it was mostly embarrassment: Mom never really wanted all eyes on her, and especially not when she was ill. Still, that's pretty much what had happened; some of her friends had seen her around town during some of her least stable moments. A couple of her closest confidantes had taken phone calls from her that were incoherent enough to pique their concern.

So she was alone. A lot.

And then there was the car wreck.

My soon-to-be ex-husband, Adam, came over to my rented condo to break the news. I hadn't answered my phone (likely because I was *in flagrante delicto* with my new love) when my family called, so they had called Adam, assuming he could still find me. Bingo. Sometime post-*delicto*, he called, persistently, until I answered. He told me he had to see me in person, that it was urgent. I thought it was more marriage drama, but he swore it was not. When he arrived at my door, he finally revealed that there had been a car wreck.

Adam told me all that he knew: Basically, everyone was fine, he said, thoroughly shaken, but fine. They'd had to use the Jaws of Life to pry Mom's car open. Everyone in it had made a trip to the hospital, but Mom and Linda would be out by the following day, and their friend Diane soon thereafter.

I wasn't sure what Adam expected. I suppose he hoped I'd need his shoulder to cry on. What I really needed was some sleep, and maybe a good hamstring massage, because I'd stressed them earlier that day. I didn't want to be mean, but he wanted me to still be in love with him. He wanted me to be weak, which I'd never been, and that was part of the whole kit and caboodle of problems we'd had. I wasn't weak this night, either, and I was tired, so I thanked him for coming to make sure I would be alright, but I assured him that I was fine, and he should go. Please. Now.

I found out as many details as I could from Casey over the phone. Mom had been driving, with Linda as a passenger, and Diane, poor thing, in the back seat of the two-door Civic I'd given Mom. It was questionable why Mom hadn't seen the vehicle that t-boned them before she made a left turn in front of it.

In a flurry of airbags and flying glass, things changed. Again.

Everyone lived. Diane had some injuries I don't recall, and Linda ended up with a shoulder problem, which later got complicated. Mom's heart changed that day, too. Not figuratively: literally. She developed a significant atrial fibrillation as a result of the accident. She stayed, again, with Linda for a while, though that was the sick nursing the sick.

Mom was tired a lot. The docs tried a couple of fancy tricks with electricity, seeing if they could shock some sense back into her ticker, but nothing seemed to hold, quite. So she added another pill to her regimen, swallowing more pharmaceuticals – something she'd never really agreed with in the first place – because it seemed like the best thing to do. Her diabetes complicated everything, so she tried to follow her doctors' orders, at least a little, perhaps for the first time in her life.

Eventually, she moved back to her apartment and was alone some more. She couldn't even have a cat there, so days must have felt endless, and she had no car now: my independent mother with her restless soul, wide-eyed and flapping.

CHAPTER 15

Christmas Trees
and
a Red Velvet Dress

I went to visit for a couple of nights just before Christmas, 2003. Mom was living in her apartment. She still would not let me sleep on the couch; she insisted I take the bed. We spent most of our days at Linda's, and evenings at her place when she felt tired.

My divorce had been final for nearly a year, and William's was final, at last, too. We'd flown from Atlanta to Los Angeles, where his parents lived, that Thanksgiving, and I'd met pretty much everyone with whom he shared blood: parents, aunts, uncles, cousins, and on and on. It was vaguely overwhelming, but we were in a hotel just up the road from his parents' house, so we didn't have the added pressure of staying with family. All in all, it

217

seemed to go fine, and I wasn't thrown out on my ear or asked not to return.

By Christmastime, though, both of us heading to Florida was impractical, and most of his vacation time was exhausted, so I made a quick trip down alone. When I think back now, I might have stayed a day or two longer had I not been so in love. William and I have always been tight-knit, but in the early days, every hour I was without him, I felt like I was longing for air. I never trusted that he would be mine for long, so I needed to breathe him in all at once in case he should disappear.

William and I had already made plans to spend our spring vacation the next year in Florida, somewhere near my hometown, so for this Christmas visit, I needed to focus on my family. And I did. By the time I boarded the plane at Tampa International to head home to Atlanta again, I was hoarse. That's how it was with Mom and me, and Linda, and Becky, too. We always had something to talk about, always had a story to share – not idle gossip, usually, but real stories: How the fig tree was lost last winter. The raccoon that had taken up residence under a local dumpster. The alligator that was found in the middle of 4th Street again. How a neighbor's cat caught a bat and let it loose in the house. Events, happenings, things to give names to.

Mom seemed well enough. There's that word again: enough. That probably explains my unease at seeing her looking grayer, older, thinner. *Was she* well enough? What was being withheld from me? Anything? Would I ever know? Linda kept her finger on the pulse of things. She took Mom to most of her doctor appointments, which surely felt to Mom ridiculous in number compared to the years she didn't go at all. For all intents and purposes, Mom was okay. There was a weird benign growth on one shoulder that, in the right top, made her look like she had on a 1980s-sized shoulder pad that had wrinkled in on itself in the wash, but it didn't hurt, she said.

We talked about Adam and about William, about how my business was frozen, a surprising development that had happened almost overnight, and about how I was getting by in the meantime with a corporate job. We talked about a little of everything, including Dad. And Carl. We even talked a little about her health, but that was never a topic she'd linger on for long. Too many words there, even for a woman who loved words, and these words didn't comprise a story, just a list: diabetes, insulin, Coumadin, a-fib, open ulcer, hyperbaric oxygen, carpal tunnel.

She didn't find those words interesting.

We talked and talked when I visited, as if we never spoke on the phone, although we still did, nearly every day. And we went to movies. We loved going to movies together, especially the good ones that get released around Christmas.

I could tell when I was with her that she still battled depression, but that was nothing new, and at the holidays, it was to be expected, counted on as much as a fat old man in a red suit. She gave me some things when I was at her apartment: her cameo, a charm, her charm bracelet. I thought little of it, but was grateful to have the items I'd played with long ago while sitting at her dressing table, dreaming of the day I'd be old enough to wear them.

I slept there in her small apartment on my last night in town, because I wanted her to feel like she was at home, a place where family felt comfortable. I lay in her bedroom that night in the dim light of an alarm clock, looking around, with joy and deep sadness, at the little that remained that was familiar.

I headed back to Atlanta on Christmas Eve, happy and lucky to have someone to come home to, eager to breathe him in again. I assured Mom, shortly before leaving, that William was truly "the best guy," and that she needn't worry, she'd meet him soon. Gray skies were gonna clear up; April, after all, was just around the corner.

And so it was. By the time February was upon us, William and I decided to move in together when our leases were up; the hunt for cohabitation was on. We found a house to rent and slowly began to funnel our things, each at our own pace, into the home that we'd share. The big final move-in date was in late April, so we'd put our journey to Florida off until sometime in May, once things were unpacked. We were happy – incredibly so – but there was absolutely no talk of marriage on the table, so what would be the rush?

It was about 4:00 in the afternoon on a Wednesday. I'd knocked off work early, though I don't remember why. I'd gone to William's place to hang out until he got home. I remember that his roommate had already moved out, so we had plans together for dinner and a bit of whatnot, I imagine. It was hard to be under two roofs when the promise of being under one was so near. I was unwinding, watching his television, which was on the floor by then. I think the roommate took the TV table in moving preparations, or maybe we'd already moved it. When my cell phone rang, it was around 4:15, and my heart leapt, thinking it was him calling to say he'd managed to break away early.

Au contraire.

As I stood in the only corner of the apartment where my cell phone had decent reception, it took me a minute to realize that it was a call from my hometown. Mom and Linda were both programmed into my cell phone. 727 had to be family. And it was: my brother Casey.

Poor Casey. What an unfortunate task. I think it began with him calling me Sue. Might've been Susan, but I think it was Sue. I hated that name, still.

"Sue, it's Casey. Are you at work?" That didn't sound good.

"Oh. Hey! No. I'm, um – at home. Well, at my boyfriend's. Why? What's . . .?"

I think he asked me to sit. What I did was kneel, what with sparse furniture and all.

Mom was dead.

Punch. Slash. Screeching wheels. Shattering glass. Wrecking ball.

Sledgehammer.

Darkness.

"Oh, no" is all I remember saying for a really long time while I cried. I wanted to know more, but I was so afraid to ask. I cried until I was brave enough. "Was it . . . I mean, Casey, did she . . .?" I thought about the things she'd given me. "She didn't kill herself, did she? Please –"

"No. No, she didn't. It looks like she probably had a heart attack. Something in the night. Linda hadn't heard from her this morning when they were supposed to do something, so she asked me to go over with her –"

Sobbing.

And then no words. None at all. Finally, I told him I'd call him back later. He made me assure him that I was okay. I did all of the reasonable things, like calling William to let him know. Like climbing, eventually, from being a lump on the carpet to being a lump on the couch. Like going to get a bath towel to blow my nose because I knew there simply were not enough Kleenex, not in all of Atlanta.

How could I be glad that she hadn't killed herself, when the fact was that she was dead?

The crying did not end that day, and the crying did not end the next. Even as we barreled down Interstate 75 toward the eventual goodbye, my tears threatened to hydroplane us off the road. Of course, William was driving. The radio played the Goo Goo Dolls' "Name," and I cried until there was no snot left in my head. He put his hand on me, and he looked at me kindly, but he did not tell me that it was alright.

I had been right about what I had told my mom: He was the best guy. He was such a good guy that he stood there beside me with the awful task of meeting every last one of my relatives as they mourned the loss of the matriarch, Jonelle. He was steadfast, a soldier: unblinking, unwavering, silent and accepting of the task laid upon him. Cloaked in solitude, he stood in service to those he did not know.

My mom had always said, when I was younger, that she wanted to be buried in a red velvet dress, and that instead of flowers, there should be Christmas trees (blue spruce, Scotch pine, Fraser fir).

She never, ever, owned a red velvet dress, that I knew of. And by the time she'd hit 40 or so, cremation was much more to her liking.

So we had a cremation, and we had a memorial service, with all of the little ceramic Christmas trees we could find. None of our pocketbooks were rich enough for a blue spruce in St. Petersburg, Florida in April. I was so glad when I saw Becky because she had remembered the Christmas tree thing, too, and brought what she could.

I managed to speak (and to choke up, and to speak a little more) at Mom's service. All the words she'd given me – how could I fail to give them back? So I did my best and read aloud a poem, "Uma," that I'd written for her many years before. Because there were no new poems in the vacuum of her loss.

Later, all of us sat in Linda's living room and wept and talked and wept and laughed, all of us, about her love, about her mad wisdom.

We laughed about too many avocadoes, and her trying to feed the family rabbit stew for dinner.

We remembered the absence of the son who'd broken her heart.

We rejoiced at the memory of her chasing our goose, which was to be Christmas dinner, into the neighbor's yard with a hatchet.

We counted, using all of our many collective fingers, the times we remembered her running out of gas.

CHAPTER 16

Remains

S orting out what remained of her belongings
was simple. We held the things we picked up
at her apartment gently, afraid to grab, to want
too much. We offered every object to each other,
afraid to strip away any memory stored in this thing
or that. There were a few figurines – Kwan Yin with
a broken hand, an old man with a broken fishing
pole – both I'd given her whole, both I took home
broken – and a tiny metal bull, a tiny carved
wooden bulldog, mala beads.

And it ended there. No more stuff.

No more. Stuff.

Her cremated remains were not ready until some
days after William had driven me, in long, silent
hours, back home. My brother scattered them.
Somehow, I'd never made it clear that I wanted any;
I'd always assumed I'd be sent some, but they were
scattered without me.

Another lesson, I assumed, from postmortem
Mom, about letting go of stuff. Ashes to ashes.

Another lesson that the stuff – all of it, all those years – did not cushion life for my mom.

I have moved like a gypsy for most of my adult life, perhaps in order to avoid the weight of things. My job history shows it; my address book most certainly does. My accumulated belongings and William's fill less than a 26-foot truck. Every time I move, I get rid of things.

And I gather no moss.

A few years ago, I was working with a bartender – one of the maddest women I've ever had the pleasure to meet – named Eden, an unbound spirit, a motorcycle-riding, tattooed, badass, Michigan hot chick. The lady's just this side of crazy, and every bit as wonderful as she sounds. She'd just moved back in with a guy she'd lived with before. They ran so hot and cold that she was worried she'd move out again, and she told me, "I'm not stressing it. It's alright. Everything I own I can fit into ten boxes."

"Boxes?"

"Well, ten of them big carrying things: Those plastic storage bins, you know? But basically, they're boxes. Everything I own can fit into ten boxes. Then if I have to go, the hell with it, I just go. I can lift all my own stuff. Nothing holding me down. Just me. Just ten boxes."

I thought about my mom:

The years and years and years of stuff.

The mountains upon mountains that were moved, every time she moved.

The weight of each child she bore, whose actions she carried throughout life as her own.

The weight of her weariness.

I thought about puzzles and books and stereopticons, fabric and buttons and magazines stacked ceiling-high, tables and papier-mâché dolls and teddy bears, grooming kits, beads, and boxes upon boxes of glow sticks.

The Stack of greeting cards.

And chocolate. Orange chocolate that smelled like urine.

I thought about every goddamned good intention she ever had, which all got buried somewhere in her stuff. And I thought about how we stripped her of it: At the end, she had so little left.

I wondered if that's how – whether that's why – she flew away.

She was never of this earth, and finally, there was nothing holding her down.

ACKNOWLEDGEMENTS

To my early readers: Elizabeth Hatch, Mary Pinizzotto, Gabrielle Cheek, Allison Zehnder, Lacy Wheeler, Deidre Dickerson, Margaret Walters, Amanda Harris, Carol Groves, Gail Westerfield and Casey Sheppard. Thank you. Your eyes were a safe place to begin.

To my editor, Gail Westerfield: Thank you for reminding me that words are music. This would be a lesser book without you.

To Mary Pinizzotto: In a nutshell-eggshell-seashell, I'll see you at the park bench under the Bonsai tree, old friend. Thanks for decades of support.

To Mark Gardiner: Thank you for your advice and encouragement. It steels my convictions.

To my dream "launch" team: You are my lucky stars. There are not enough words to thank you for your willingness to climb aboard.

To Binders, far and wide: You are an endless inspiration. Thank you.

To my husband, friends, and family: You give me stories worth telling, and the courage to tell them honestly. I only hope for more. I love you.

ABOUT THE AUTHOR

Susan Fekete is a lifelong student, curious about everything that the world has to teach. Her insatiable desire for learning blossomed into in a nomadic lifestyle; she's lived in two countries, five states, and thirty-two different homes, and her career has spanned nine different industries - three of them as an entrepreneur. She has a broad perspective on being human and is always dreaming about her next great adventure and how she'll write about it.

A native Floridian and graduate of Florida State University's School of Theatre, she currently resides in majestic Sonoma County, California with her husband, William, and their beloved dog.

.

CPSIA information can be obtained
at www.ICGtesting.com
Printed in the USA
FSHW02n0038170518
48058FS